Lost Secrets
of the
Mystery Schools

The Coming of the Gods
Initiation and Rebirth

Earlyne Chaney, Ph.D.

Astara's Library of Mystical Classics

Published by

Astara

800 W. Arrow Highway
Upland, CA 91786

Cover Design: Steve Doolittle

Printed in the United States of America

Dedication

From the depths of my heart I lovingly dedicate this book to Phyllis Harrison, my secretarial assistant, without whose skill, tenacity and devotion this book would never have been completed. This gentle soul who is so purified in her loyalty dances with the infinite as a true child of light and there she shall reap her reward—an immeasurable expression of my love and gratitude.

Acknowledgments

With deep gratitude I acknowledge the steadfast efforts of my devoted "computer secretary," Phyllis Harrison, and her assistant, Fran Blaye, whose skills, knowledge and devotion have made this book possible. Also, I thank Dawn and Neal McKenzie for their untiring efforts throughout Greece, Ephesus and Medjugorje to obtain photographs to be used in this and other books, and in their dedicated efforts to produce videotapes of these journeys. Without the efforts of these wonderful people these words may never have been. And if these words of gratitude are but a moment in the flow of eternity then I shall be eternally grateful to each who has contributed so very much.

Other Books by Earlyne Chaney

Remembering—The Autobiography of a Mystic
The Masters and Astara
Secrets From Mount Shasta
The Book of Beginning Again
Revelations of Things to Come
Beyond Tomorrow—a Book of Prophecies
Shining Moments of a Mystic
Initiation in the Great Pyramid
Forever Young
The YOU Book—A Treasury of Health and Healing

****

Published by Samuel Weiser, Inc.

The Mystery of Death and Dying—
Initiation at the Moment of Death
The Eyes Have It

****

Astara's Book of Life
A series of esoteric teachings of the
Mystery Schools of all ages

****

Books in Collaboration

Kundalini and the Third Eye
With William Messick
The Mystical Marriage of Science and Spirit
By Frances Paelian
(Based on the teachings of Earlyne Chaney)

TABLE OF CONTENTS

INTRODUCTION

When one first turns one's thoughts toward Greece, whether in anticipation of a journey there or just in a flashback of meditative awareness, one is apt to indulge in only a casual conception of the ancient islands and temples, curiosity concerning the incredible weaving still done by the peasantry, and anticipation of the bargains in fur products—especially the fur coats—with a slight interest toward today's industries, the progression of Greece and the political environment—with smatterings, of course, of the history of bygone eras.

The Acropolis rises 156 m. above sea level to dominate the entire city of Athens. Once a fortress, it is inaccessible from all sides except the west side where the entrance is located. Under the influence of Pericles, the "high city" became a religious center. The Parthenon housed the magnificent statue of Athena, goddess and protectress of the city. Even in majestic ruins, the Parthenon today bears witness to the glory that was Greece.

But the light seeker's conception is considerably different. Secondary are thoughts of the politics, the industry and the bargains in merchandise. The mystic looks forward to visiting or studying about the important sites of the ancient Mystery Schools, viewing the ruins of the majestic temples firsthand and establishing an etheric link to ancient memories—the initiations of long ago, the Academy of Plato, the Lyceum of Aristotle; to tread the pathways of the great philosophers of antiquity, and Mount Olympus, home of the twelve gods and goddesses who came to Greece from outer space.

The mystic wants to pay homage to those ancient gods, our ancestors, and to the immortal souls who departed Greece to be initiated in the Mystery Schools in the golden land of Egypt—then returned to establish their own Mystery Schools in Greece. In this present writing the history of Greece will be sought only as it relates to the mysteries of the past and the pathways of the initiates, to their Mystery Schools of antiquity and their subtle but unmistakable influence upon modern-day Mystery Schools.

As in all sites of antiquity, archaeologists and historians separate the past into particular periods. The historical past for Greece began about 3,000 years before the coming of Christ, which has been labeled the Bronze Age. But we mystics hold subconscious memories of an age much earlier—the time of Atlantis, and even to the sinking of the last remnants of that wondrous land around 13,000 years ago.

And we know quite well that some measure of civilization can be traced as far back as 100,000 years ago. We know because tombs have been found which give evidence that the dead were buried in a sacred manner at least that long ago. These early Eartheans lived as nomadic tribes, following herds of animals as they sought grazing pastures. These wanderers worshiped nature spirits, the devas. To them the landscape, the trees, the flowing water, the mountain tops, even the flowers were endowed with spiritual essences which eventually acquired human qualities, personalities, powers and attributes.

The earliest evidence of habitation in the Greek world goes beyond prehistoric times. It's an axe made of greenish trachyte measuring 15.3 cm. long and 10 cm. wide. It was discovered in the village of Paleocastro near Siatista in 1963. It's at least 100,000 years old. Other discoveries clearly indicate the area was inhabited as early as the lower Paleolithic Age, between 100,000 and 40,000 B.C. But the most significant find was the skull of a Neanderthal woman near the village of Petralona in the Chalcidice peninsula. She lived some time between 70,000 and 60,000 B.C. Clearly, Neanderthal types wandered the land until about 40,000 years ago, when this entire race of beings suddenly disappeared to be replaced overnight by Homo sapien, types of humans, who aren't too different from us today.

What happened to the Neanderthals? Where did the Homo sapiens suddenly come from about 40,000 B.C.? Did the space beings arriving on Earth intermarry so quickly among the Neanderthals, the Neanderthals were absorbed as a race and as such ceased to exist?—or did the space gods take the Neanderthals to another planet for further evolution? Or did the space people engage in genetic engineering by artificial insemination?—did they take sperm from Neanderthal beings and link it to the ovum of some space goddess to bring forth a new breed of man? Did they take ovum from some Neanderthal woman and link it to sperm from a space god to bring forth a new breed of woman?

Through such birthings, the Neanderthals *could* disappear overnight. And a new race of Earthean could suddenly appear— just as they did. Homo sapiens were suddenly here, and civilization took a tremendous leap forward not only in Greece but in Egypt, in Mesoamerica, in Tibet and all over the Earth. Some of the Neanderthals must have been left because even now there is a sharp division in the human race—some are highly developed spiritual-intellectual "star" people while some are barely beyond the primitive state. We walk side by side in our present state of progression.

So let's let our memories take us back to the days when the gods and goddesses of space first visited our planet. They came to promote a leap in evolution for the lifewave of souls struggling to progress on Earth. Perhaps they came from Sirius, perhaps from the Pleiades, or Orion, perhaps from other planets or stars. Viewing this incredibly beautiful Earth planet from their space-ships, twelve special gods and goddesses chose a mount in Greece for one of their most incomparable headquarters. They labeled it Mount Olympus. Even prior to that time others had already landed in Egypt. Isis, Osiris and Horus had established the Mystery Schools. Hermes had, perhaps, even built the pyramids.

The twelve who settled on Mount Olympus were really fourteen: Zeus, the leader, Apollo, Athena, Poseidon, Artemis, Demeter, Hephaestos, Hera, Aphrodite, Dionysus, Ares, Hermes—and Hestia, goddess of the hearth, and Hades, brother of Zeus, who was consigned to the netherworld. Hades, however, played a prominent role in the Mysteries. He was also known as Pluto. Above all there was always Gaea, the Mother Goddess. "One race there is of men and one of gods, but from one mother, Earth, draw we both our breath." Athena, Demeter, Artemis, Hera, and Aphrodite each drew attributes from the always over-shadowing Gaea, Mother Nature herself. Hermes was equally renowned in both Greece and Egypt. Zeus, long before, had ap-peared on Crete, an island near the mainland, to begin building its incredible civilization. Only after Crete was established did he establish Mount Olympus on the mainland of Greece.

So, let's explore some of the inner mysteries of these great beings whose forms were parallel with perfection. And whose wisdom reached far beyond our present-day understanding. Let us view each of them not as myth and legend, but as celestial personalities who came from a faraway planet to impart knowl-edge and wisdom to the primitive peoples of Earth.

1. Zeus   7. Hephaestos
2. Apollo   8. Hera
3. Athena   9. Aphrodite
4. Poseidon 10. Dionysus
5. Artemis 11. Ares
6. Demeter 12. Hermes
            13. Hestia
            14. Hades - Pluto
            15. Gaea

Chapter One

The Coming of the Mystery Schools

From what distant star did the space gods arrive?

In this present writing, my words will be directed toward bringing to life the gods and goddesses that the historians, the scientists and the mythologists have been busily burying under centuries of scientific data to make of them only subconscious levels of the mind. We want to restore them as living, thinking and creative beings whose attributes have been subtly interwoven in the subconscious mind of all humankind. So vividly are they entwined in our subconscious they are forever linking us to a forgotten past, raising us to a higher dimension of consciousness, and attuning us to the wisdom that still seeps into our souls like the ethers of an onflowing airwave of light.

Throughout the ages since their arrival on Earth the Greek gods and goddesses have indeed become humanized. Is it because they are our ancestors? Is it because they parented a portion of humankind? Is it because they came to Earth

1

to seed the barbaric hordes of Earth's humanity? And is it because of them that today we bear both the seeds of divinity and humanness? Did they give us the seeds of divinity, of mind? What was humanity on Earth like before the coming of the gods?

Only the light seeker will establish them as beings of reality. We enter that long ago memory and attunement with our souls longing to remember more, because perhaps some of us lived in Greece during the days when the gods and goddesses walked that majestic land. Perhaps we sat in their Mystery Schools and were taught the wisdom they came to share.

Coming into rebirth in this modern day, and again becoming initiates in some modern Mystery School, arouses within us such a longing we reach back to remember more vividly the arrival of the spaceships which brought those great beings to Earth. We see in our mind's eye the immortal twelve, with their leader Zeus, as they arrived from some distant star. Other beings had already arrived in other locations all over the planet. There were Isis, Osiris and Horus in Egypt, and the incomparable monolithic Great Pyramid of Giza. There were Odin and Baldur the Beautiful in Scandinavia, with their thunderbolts. There were King Arthur, Merlin and the Knights of the Round Table in England, holding council in their now-vanished Camelot. There was Vishnu in India; Quetzalcoatl in South America, who left behind a civilization which built the enigmatic pyramids of Mesoamerica— Chichen Itza, Copan, Palenque in the Yucatan. There were the Incas who landed on the Island of the Sun in Lake Titicaca in Bolivia, who built the incredible walls of the fortress of Sacsahuaman, the Temple of the Sun inside those walls, and the incomparable solid gold Punchao altar which adorned one complete wall of that magnificent temple in Peru. Many of the stones of those astonishing walls weighed as much as 20,000 tons each, and fitted together so perfectly not even a thin knife blade could penetrate their joints. They built and then suddenly deserted the mysterious lost city of Machu Picchu, also in Peru. And there were so many others....

Osiris   *Isis*   *Horus*

So much evidence indicates that the gods and goddesses were here one would have to be blind not to be aware of it. There is the calendar found in the mud of the ancient city of Tiahuanaco near Lake Titicaca, where ruins rise 13,500 feet above the level of the Pacific, near the frontier of Bolivia high in the Andes mountains. The calendar obviously was made by superior beings, giving the rotation of Earth, the equinoxes, the astronomical seasons, and the movements and tides of the moon. And there stands the astonishing Gate of the Sun, an enormous monolith thirteen feet five inches long, seven feet high and eighteen inches thick, carved from a single block weighing more than 10 tons. Once the trachyte of which it was constructed shone like highly polished gold.

On the lintel beam is carved what could be a cosmonaut—a flying god—surrounded by forty-eight companions. Before all these, there were the beings who first established Lemuria, then Atlantis.

The Mystery Schools of Greece

After establishing Mystery Schools all over the planet and sharing much of their knowledge—after begetting sons and daughters, the demigods, to carry on the traditions—the great ones departed Earth. In this writing I focus on only one country—Greece—where the gods and goddesses established the ancient culture of a nation which became part of the magic and mysticism of the entire world.

After many ages, as the Mystery Schools they established sank further into oblivion—because the souls of Earth were not prepared to carry on that secret wisdom—the reality of the gods and the goddesses of Greece faded and the myths of these person-alities took on a legendary quality as if they had not existed. Even-tually historians and psychologists caused them to represent some phase of nature which had been personalized, or innate qualities of the soul. But the light seeker knows they were living, breathing entities possessing both human and divine qualities. They came to give Eartheans a fragment of their own divinity. And we know that Mount Olympus truly existed as the home of these god be-ings.

The twelve eventually were regarded as embodying the full attributes of God in that Greek religion included swearing by them as one swears by God himself. "I swear by the twelve," meaning the twelve gods of Olympus. The indiscreet activities attributed to the gods can, with insight, be interpreted as symbolic of secrets of initiation which could never be revealed to the profane.

With the arrival of the space people in Greece, primitive life was quickly left far behind—just as it happened all over the plan-et. In Egypt with the arrival of Imhotep. In South America with the coming of Quetzalcoatl. In Mesoamerica with the coming of

Viracocha, Lord Maru and the first Inca. In India with the teachings of the Rishis.

The gods in Greece encouraged the tribal worship of the gods of nature which they made visible in their temples, in sculpture and in drama. These sacred temples dotted entire landscapes, establishing a bold testimony to their belief in devas or nature spirits, in a Mother Earth goddess and the presence of a divine god of space. Sites of their temples were selected through their knowledge of electromagnetic currents of unseen force, patterned after the etheric gridwork of the planet.

The leap forward in civilization has often been called "the Greek miracle." Exactly when it happened no one really knows. We only know Greece suddenly leaped from a tribal nomadic primitive state with Neanderthal man to become the cultural center of the world. The same thing happened in Egypt during the Third Dynasty, in the reign of King Zoser. Suddenly there was Imhotep, and suddenly there was an incomparable wisdom side by side with the primitives of Earth—a remarkable civilization entwined with the silent sphinx and the monument to the gods— the Great Pyramid, inscrutable House of the Hidden Places, the Mysteries and initiation—and Thoth-Hermes.

In the eighth century, Hesiod, a poor peasant farmer in Greece composed a theogony describing the creation of man and his separation from his gods. Writing under direct inspiration of one of the gods, he left for posterity a history of humanity. He established the idea that humankind had been in a steady state of decline, rather than that of progressive evolution. He taught that mankind once existed in a state of grace, but fell from it out of disobedience—very like the tradition of our biblical Genesis. He describes the spiritual state called the Golden Age when human beings dwelt in etheric realms, probably much like our Garden of Eden—from which they fell into the world of matter, the physical condition.

Hesiod then described a Silver Age in which humanity, fallen from a spiritual state, became the primitive of Earth, void of true understanding of Earth, heaven and God. This early man set up altars in selected places to offer worship to his gods and he frequently burnt offerings. Often gods or "angels" appeared at these places and man was purified by the encounter. These men, however, loved war and violence and were constantly destroying themselves. Hesiod's cosmogony brings man to his own era. He established the possibility that humanity may yet contact the gods and emerge into a reflected state of salvation.

The theogony of Hesiod included information about the Olympian gods and goddesses. He described them as divine beings who came from "the sky." Although they were not supreme and worked under a higher being, they were immortal in that they had mastered the art of transmuting their physical forms into etheric forms and of dwelling simultaneously in our world of matter and in higher etheric realms. His cosmogony describes the union of the Sky Father with the Earth Mother. Could he possibly have been speaking of the space beings who came and chose "the fairest of Earth" to wed as described in Biblical scripture? Could he have been referring to the genetic engineering of linking the reproductive substances of the gods and goddesses of space with the grosser substances of the early Earthean—to bring forth a new creature?

Imhotep was builder of the Step Pyramid of King Zoser in Egypt's Third Dynasty. He was also chancellor, sage, god of medicine, astronomer and demigod.

Hesiod's cosmogony, with its revelation of spaceships and space beings, brings to mind the great epic of the Hindus, The Mahabharata. The Mahabharata describes the vimanas of antiquity—their flying ships—when the space people came to Earth eons ago and landed in India. This epic poem describes a battle involving the UFOs or vimanas of those early eons. Perhaps these space people, with their vimanas, came from Atlantis—or from some star system deep in space first, to Atlantis, then to India. The poem establishes that tens of thousands of years ago there existed on Earth a civilization more technically advanced than ours—that possessed spaceships capable of traveling far afield— not only to other planets, but to other solar systems.

Another epic poem of the Hindus, called the Ramayana also describes the vimanas, the massive spaceships. The Ramayana speaks of the god Rama and Sita, his beloved wife, who was abducted by Raven. Taking Sita with him, Raven directed his spaceship toward the city of Ranka, pursued by Rama. There followed a long war to free Sita. During the battle, Rama finally used "the dart of Endra," a terrible weapon which could slay 10,000 men with its "thunderbolt." Could this be the same type of "thunderbolt" Zeus possessed in Greece? And Thor in Scandinavia? The "weapons" of all three were called lightning bolts and thunderbolts.

Another stanza describes how Rama brought Raven low with the rays of his thunderbolt and rescued Sita. The weapons of Rama, Zeus and Thor are too similar to be ignored. Obviously spaceships were used in the battle of Rama-Sita-Raven. And some sort of laser death ray—the thunderbolt.

Zeus with his thunderbolt controlled his area of the world from Mt. Olympus. The space travelers with Zeus set up communities usually apart from the tribes of Earth. Those that chose to settle in Greece chose Mt. Olympus as their headquarters. Evidence points to Earth's Mt. Olympus as only the touchpoint of the space people on Earth. The real Mt. Olympus was in the etheric realms, lying over and about the physical plane Mt. Olympus. And the

The Mighty Zeus.
He holds a weapon in his
upraised hand—possibly
his laser thunderbolt.

gods and goddesses, being immortal, could easily depart the etheric Olympus and appear on Earth's Mt. Olympus, transmuting their etheric form to that of the physical. Their etheric abode was a place of perfect blessedness. Their earthly abode—Mt. Olympus—only served as a place apart from the primitive tribes of Earth.

If one insists on placing a date for the arrival of the gods upon Olympus, a possible date could be 40,000 years ago, with the latest arriving 5,000 years ago. Their Olympus headquarters were firmly established before the sinking of Atlantis and they begat several offspring prior to the time history began. Space beings returned about 5,000 years ago in Egypt, during the Third Dynasty when King Zoser reigned.

For our particular research relating to Greece, the Minoans settled on the island of Crete between 4000 and 3000 B.C. There they founded an astonishing civilization, Europe's first. Their civilization rose in glory long before the mainland of Greece began to be recognized as a civilization.

King Minos of Crete was the son of Zeus and Europa—a demigoddess of Europe. Europa was the lovely princess after whom the continent is named. The peace and progression of both

Crete and the mainland was disrupted by the eruption of the volcano of Thera, a nearby island and Cretan colony, about 1450 B.C. Today many people believe that Thera, now called Santorini, is part of the lost island of Atlantis. Recent discoveries point to that possibility. A whole city has recently been excavated from beneath 160 feet of lava and pumice. After this stupendous eruption which disrupted the civilization of Crete, the mainland of Greece rapidly began its development.

Throughout all those early centuries there continued a tradition of worship centered on the Sky Gods, chief of whom was Zeus. The worship was counterbalanced by worship centered on the Earth Mother Goddess. There gradually emerged a marriage of these Sky-Earth gods. With the passing of the ages and the intermarriages of the Sky Gods with Earth's fairest maidens, civilization came to be recorded as history about 3000 B.C., the Bronze Age. The Sky Gods had long since departed, leaving a strain of their divinity in the bloodstream and the genes of developing humankind.

The Coming of the Mystery Schools

Many who have attempted to trace the source of the Mystery Schools have placed their beginnings in the Garden of Eden. They insist the fig leaf was the first apron worn by these early initiates. Others declare that the Mystery Schools were brought from other planets when space beings arrived on Earth to teach Eartheans the mysteries of God, the soul, the spirit, the universe and creation, evolution and immortality. It is quite obvious this is true. But the difficulty lies in establishing where the first Mystery Schools had their beginnings. Proof of such research is inconsequential.

It is obvious that the earliest among our records were established in Egypt. Ancient history tells us that the civilization of Egypt was far advanced when other nations were just emerging from barbarism. Her Mysteries, mythology and symbolism were well established so that other societies of antiquity copied all of them. Those seeking true initiation journeyed from far away sites to be initiated in Egypt.

The erudite priesthood there achieved comprehensive results to preserve the divine truths of religion on Earth. We must lean upon tradition to obtain glimpses of the incomparable wisdom of early Egypt. There, religion blended with the affairs of daily life. The Mysteries constituted the instruction towards which mortals strove to fulfill their physical and moral welfare.

The Mysteries of Egypt attracted the wisest and most spiritual souls from all nations who carried the Egyptian wisdom back to their own lands. It is no secret that the great philosophers of Greece all journeyed first to Egypt. Hebrew-Christianity owes to Egypt its concept of the deity. Egyptian inscriptions pointing toward such knowledge were made centuries before Moses received the tablets of law on the summit of Sinai. In the hieroglyphs of Egypt can be found ancient observations on the heavenly bodies, made twenty-five hundred years before Galileo presented his theory of planetary revolution.

The Egyptian Mysteries

The Egyptian Mysteries embraced the doctrine of cosmogony (the science of the origin and development of the universe). The Mysteries also included astronomy, the arts, sciences and religion which led toward the immortality of the soul. Through impressive rites and ceremonies they led their neophytes from darkness to light, from ignorance to knowledge, from knowledge to wisdom.

Even in those early days the Mysteries were divided. The Lesser were offered to the multitudes, the Greater only to the candidates for the priesthood. Realizing many neophytes could never attain the Greater, the priesthood used symbols adapted to that purpose. Thus there evolved a symbolic language in which the priesthood concealed the real truths of the Mysteries.

The drama of the Mysteries presented the tragic death of Osiris, the search for his body by Isis, the goddess of the moon and the queen of the ocean. It revolved around the discovery of the body of Osiris by Isis and its restoration to life and power.

The attack of Typhon, the brother of Osiris, and the spirit of darkness and evil, was enacted amid terrible scenes during which the judgements of the dead and the punishments suffered by the wicked were represented as realities to the neophyte. This drama was conducted as a means of revealing to even a neophyte the truth of the initiation at the moment of death. Following the slaying of Osiris by Typhon, his body was at last found by Isis, his widow, concealed in a mysterious chest. After much sorrow and despair Osiris was returned to life and power amid effulgent beams of light radiating from the goddess Isis. And through his resurrection the initiates were shown the resplendent plains of Paradise.

Even the dramas of Lesser Mysteries represented a mystical death and descent into the infernal regions where sin was purged by the elements and the initiate was regenerated and restored to a life of light and purity.

The Greater Mysteries involved actually placing the initiate in a state of symbolic death for a period of three days, during which his or her spirit soared aloft to gain wisdom of the actual death transition. There is no question but that the mysterious soma drink helped to bring the candidate to that trance state—and the use of the drink was part of the secret ritual of initiation.

The early Mysteries were celebrated once a year when candidates were initiated into three degrees. The first was entitled *Isis*, the second, *Serapis*, and the third, *Osiris*. At the time of initiation each candidate was required to make a full confession of all dark events occurring in his or her life. In the first degree a guide took charge of the neophyte, conducting him/her down a long, dark passage to a subterranean chamber where s/he met the dwellers on the threshold of death. S/he also was asked certain questions, the answers to which enabled him/her to proceed toward higher chambers. In this ascent s/he was subjected to severe trials. At the conclusion of the initiation s/he was required to take a solemn and binding oath of secrecy and fidelity.

In the second degree s/he represented the principal attributes of the Judge of the Dead and the Keeper of Hades. This degree, like the first, prepared the candidate for the third by requiring answers to certain questions. There followed again severe trials at the termination of which s/he was required to take an additional vow of silence and fidelity. After a period of time during which s/he demonstrated her/his integrity, the initiate was granted the third or highest degree. In this degree s/he represented Osiris. As Osiris s/he experienced the ceremony of death itself and later her/his resurrection. Again, at the conclusion of this highest degree, s/he took a final vow: "May my departed spirit wander into eternal mystery without a place of rest should I ever violate the obligations conferred upon me by the hierophants of the Sacred Mysteries."

Out of these Greater Mysteries came the initiates known as *the Builders* who actually became architects and builders of tem-

from the Manly P. Hall Collection,
copyright Philosophical Research Society.

The Ptah or Hierophant first placed the initiate in a state of hypnotic trance—after which he or she lay in a state of suspended animation for three days, during which the soul escaped the confines of the body to sojourn in the celestial spheres. Upon awakening, the new initiate-hierophant understood the mystery of death itself, of initiation of the soul into the Clear Light of salvation at the moment of death, and life on the otherside.

ples and splendid edifices designed exclusively for the worship of deity. From these high initiates also came the rulers, the priests, the warriors and the statesmen.

The Eleusinian Mysteries

The Eleusinian Mysteries, patterned after those of Egypt, were established in Greece about 1800 B.C. When the Athenians conquered Eleusis the inhabitants willingly surrendered everything except their mythologies and Mysteries. The Eleusinian Mysteries were celebrated once a year. To make this celebration possible a most magnificent temple was erected at Eleusis. The hierophant, or high priest, clad in magnificence, sat in the East upon a resplendent throne surrounded by seven brilliant lights representing the seven sacred planets. The principal officers surrounding him were the priests at the altar, the daduchus and the herald.

Over the head of the hierophant, the Master of the Lodge, was a beautiful arch. Above it were the moon and seven stars. The twenty-four attendants, clad in white and wearing golden crowns, represented the twenty-four ancient constellations of the upper hemisphere.

Isis, who led the procession in search of the lost body of Osiris, represented the moon. The daduchus was the torchbearer. His duty was to impose silence on the assembly and command the profane to withdraw. The priest officiated at the altar. The herald preserved order and punished all who disturbed the sacred rites.

Before a candidate was admitted for initiation he was required to pass through a period of probation, make confession, and undergo physical purification. At the time he was accepted as a candidate he was clothed in a dark robe and blindfolded. The guides conducted him through a dark and circuitous passage into a cavern where he heard the roar of wild beasts, the hiss of serpents, and was subjected to a dreadful thunderstorm, through swirling waters, terrible thunder and flashes of incredible lightning.

Emerging from this ordeal he was conducted to a massive door. Upon removal of his blindfold he read this inscription: "He who would attain to the perfect state must be purified by the three great elements." Whereupon the door slowly swung open and he was thrust into darkness. There he combatted a whirlwind.

Next, he was compelled to cross a hall, the walls of which darted flames of fire, threatening his life. Completing this ordeal, he was thrown into a dark and swift stream of water across which he had to swim or drown. If the candidate survived this test of fortitude s/he was conducted to the Great Hall of the Mysteries where, in the presence of all the assembled priests and adepts, he took the oath of fidelity and secrecy, following which he received his instructions and a benediction. He was also clothed in the appropriate robes of the first degree.

At the end of a year the initiate was invited to a higher degree. During this ceremony a sacrifice was made for the candidate and he took a higher oath of secrecy. He was then invested with a sacred cloak, mystic collars and a crown of palm leaves.

Massive ruins of Eleusis where the Eleusinian Mysteries were celebrated

At the termination of another year of probation the initiate was raised to the third degree. During these ceremonies he witnessed the death of the Master Builder, the search for his body and his resurrection. During these ceremonies he was conducted to the threshold of the labyrinth through which he made his way amid horrible scenes from which he emerged into another chamber with walls draped in black and hung with emblems of death. There he was shown, in the distance, scenes of terror and the horrors of Tartarus, or hell.

He witnessed a tragic drama in which the murder of the Master Builder was committed by three ruffians. The body of the murdered Master was laid on a bier before him. A funeral dirge was chanted and dusky phantoms led by Isis in search of the dead body passed before him. Suddenly, the body of the Master disappeared from the bier. Then a flood of dazzling light burst upon the scene and standing in its midst the awed candidate beheld the resurrected body of the murdered Master. Such a display heralded exclamations of joy and triumph. This ended the fearful ordeal. The initiate had become the adept and the brilliant scenes of the Elysian Fields and the bliss of the purified were opened before him. The ceremony concluded when the candidate was led to the altar and took again the obligations of the degree. This describes, in brief, some of the ceremonies. It does not include the rigorous training of the candidate during the years of probation nor the actual details of the inner Mysteries. It does not offer detailed description of the seven initiations which were actually involved in the three major degrees.*

The horrors exhibited at the beginning of these ceremonies represented the condition of the wicked soul. The triumphant scenes represented the abode of the blessed. The candidate was shown the miseries of Tartarus, or hell, and the happiness of Elysium, or heaven, as a means of contrast between the afterlife of the wicked and the afterlife of the good. Some of these Egyptian Mysteries were called Cabiri, meaning "powerful gods."

---

*See *Initiation in the Great Pyramid,* available at your bookstore or Astara, 800 W. Arrow Hwy., P.O. Box 5003 Upland, CA 91785-5003.

Later Mysteries

The Mysteries of the Gnostics held to the Egyptian Mysteries with elements of the Jewish and Christian traditions involved.

The Dionysian Mysteries also comprised a tragedy—a murder, a search for the body, its discovery and restoration to life. The Mithraic Mysteries were patterned after the Eleusinian Mysteries except that in addition there were seven grades, or initiations, rather than three. After completing these trying ordeals the neophyte of Mithras was presented with an engraved amulet as a token of his/her priesthood. S/he was offered a crown which s/he was expected to refuse, saying, "My only crown is Mithras." The Mysteries of Mithras found their way into Gaul, Germany and Britain. In all the Mysteries, regeneration was represented. An assassination of a great master took place, followed by a search for the body, its recovery and its resurrection. During the period of search, grief and mourning were demonstrated followed by great joy and happiness.

The Essenes

The Essenes—a secret society of Semitics who rejected orthodox Judaism—originated around 200 B.C. These initiates rose before sunrise, assembled and prayed with their faces turned toward the sun. Each candidate passed through a period of preparation and purification which extended over three years. During the first stage of his candidacy he was required to turn all of his property in to the common treasury. He was then given a copy of the ordinances, a spade, an apron and a white robe.

After the first year of probation he was admitted into the second stage, during which he enjoyed a closer fellowship with other candidates and was invited to share in more of the closed rites and ceremonies. He could not hold an office nor sit at the common table. After completion of the second stage he was admitted to the third-year rank, or third degree. Here he was required to take a solemn oath to practice charity and never to reveal the secrets of the Order.

Without doubt, Jesus was an Essene. He wore the white robe, practiced healing and demonstrated ideal purity as was required of the Essenes.

Qumran and the Dead Sea Scrolls

On a spring day in 1947, among the barren Judean foothills that rise above the northwest shore on the Dead Sea, a goat in search of greener pastures precipitated the most significant religious discovery in recent history. As a Bedouin shepherd pursued the animal he stumbled on a hidden cave which contained the first of the now famous Dead Sea Scrolls. The shepherds who had hoped for treasure were disappointed to find eight crumbling manuscripts wrapped in linen and stored in large earthen jars. In

At Qumran

Jerusalem they eventually found two buyers—the Hebrew University and the Metropolitan Jacobite Church.

Among the crumbling manuscripts was found a full text of Isaiah, commentary on Habakkuk, a collection of hymns, a scroll, tentatively thought to be the *Book of Leamech*, and a heretofore unknown work called *The War of the Children of Light Against the Children of Darkness*. The manuscripts apparently dated back to the second or third century B.C. and antedated the oldest existing Hebrew biblical manuscript by more than a thousand years.

The caves in which the original manuscript and others were found were in an area called Khirbet Qumran which is a stone ruin near the Dead Sea. Qumran was the site of an Essene establishment and it was apparent that the lost manuscripts were once a part of the Essene library and that *The War of the Children of Light* were Essene writings.

The Essenes, sometimes called the *Sect of the Covenant*, hid their library in nearby caves. The Essenes obviously had withdrawn from the orthodox Jewish religion and had actually become the first Christians. It is obvious they were followers of the Pythagorean philosophy. They practiced baptism, and the Eucharist was an important part of their religious ritual. They taught redemption of the soul and immortality, or life after death. Their sainted leader was a mysterious figure called the Teacher of Righteousness, a Messianic prophet-priest blessed with the gift of divine revelation, who was eventually persecuted and martyred. Supposedly, this teacher was our Jesus of Nazareth who ventured forth from his Essene community to teach the Essenean philosophy to both Jew and Gentile.

The ancient manuscripts contain many phrases, symbols, teachings and precepts similar to those in the New Testament, especially in the gospel of John and the Paulist Epistles. John the Baptist's use of baptism points to the fact that he too was an Essene. Pliney, the Roman statesman, says that, *Toward the west of the Dead Sea the Essenes established their communities. They are a hermitical society, marvelous beyond all others throughout the whole earth. They live without women, without money and in groves of palm trees. Their ranks are daily made up of multitudes of newcomers who resort to them and who, being weary of life and driven by the surges of ill fortune, adopt their manner of life. Thus it is that through thousands of ages, incredible to relate, those people prolonged their existence without anyone being born among them, so fruitful to them are the weary lives of others.*

The Druids

The secret doctrines, the ceremonies and the rites of the Druids were so similar to those of the ancient Egyptians that the relationship between them was obvious. One of their most striking similarities was the worship of the sun as witnessed by the great annual festival held on May 1st in honor of Belinus, or the sun. On this day the Druids always kindled prodigious fires in all their sacred places and offered sacrifices to the sun and the sun god. Their Builders erected great temples constructed on geometric and astronomical principles, often in the form of a cross and a circle. In the center of the circle a gigantic representative of the deity was always erected. Often their temples were built in the form of groves of gigantic oak trees, again with the principal oak tree in the center. Often from the central tree, voices spoke from unseen dimensions, initiating and guiding the initiates.

From Wellcome's
Ancient Cymric Medicine

Arch-Druid

The principal function of the Druids in the exoteric world was as priest-healers. They often used amulets charged with magnetism to heal, as we use crystals today. They also used the mistletoe because its substance attracted the magnetism of the astral light. It grew in abundance on their sacred oak trees. They were also renowned astronomers, gathering their herbs, mistletoe and other plants only when the sun, moon, and stars indicated.

The Druids always elected one chief or Arch-Druid to whom was given supreme authority. He commanded, decreed and punished. It was he who climbed the oak tree at a certain season of the year to cut the mistletoe with a golden sickle, which was symbolic of destroying the qualities of animalistic self.

It was in 61 A.D. when Nero sent a Roman army to destroy the power of the Druids. The Romans attacked and defeated the Britains on the isle of Anglesea. The Romans demolished their temples, overturned their altars, and burned many of the Druids in the fires which had been kindled for sacrificing. The Druids never regained power in ancient Britain.

Chapter Two

The Beginning

We stand in the midst of a sea of unknown qualities—ramifications of power, cycles of evolutionary development—and seeing, see not. The light shines all around us but we comprehend it not. We turn amusedly away from the ancient pantheons of bygone religions, ridiculing their belief in the gods and goddesses, believing that they never really existed.

The usual Westerner regards them as fantasy and without practical existence, mainly because of the misguided teachings of limited orthodox Christianity. S/he has been taught nothing concerning spiritual life except the existence of God and Christ. No provision has been made for further spiritual education. The Church fathers have called ancient religions heretic and labeled past religions as pagan. We never seem to think of the Elohim as possibly being gods or goddesses. They're simply "angels before the throne of God." We seldom consider whether or not the gods or goddesses of yore might have been renamed as the angels and archangels of Christianity.

To truly understand such a possibility, we must seek prior to the birth of Christianity. And we must probe beyond mythology to grasp the possibility of the reality of space beings among early humanity, and view those eons devoid of current concepts. What were Earth and Eartheans like prior to the coming of the gods?

When the gods and goddesses from space first arrived on Earth they were met by three types of beings: the Cyclopes, the Titans and the monsters. All were gigantic in size. The Cyclopes all had one enormous eye in the middle of the forehead. The Titans were mammoth in size, too, but most were beautiful in stature and beneficent in manner. The race of monsters was called the Giants, children of Ouranos, the Father in Heaven, and Gaea, Mother Earth, brought forth during the days when Earth was in her earliest formation, and physical bodies were not yet ready to receive the souls of human inhabitants.

The Cyclopes

Most were benevolent, but some were of a warlike nature. Some were skilled at stone masonry, others as blacksmiths and as shepherds. The stone masons were extremely skilled, having built the enormous wall around Mycenae which is, even now, called the Cyclopean Wall. Those who were skilled as blacksmiths were employed by Zeus to manufacture his thunderbolts. This means that they were acquainted with creating a laser weapon or were capable of being instructed in such an art.

An article, published in 1989, proclaims that Japanese scientists recently found the skull of a Cyclopes on an island in the South Pacific. According to their report the skull was found in a shallow grave on the island of Kadavu, about 60 miles south of Fiji, on September 21, 1989. The skull is clearly marked with an enormous eye in the middle of the forehead.

The scientists declare that the one-eyed creature died sometime during World War II. They declare that the skull is not a fossil. Believing it to be thousands of years old they were stunned to discover that the Cyclopes died between 1941 and 1944. Its size indicates that it belonged to a creature at least eight feet tall. The archaeologist in charge of the discovery is Isao Fujita of Ja-

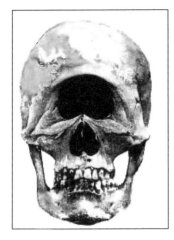

pan. Dr. Fujita and his associate, Isamil Nogami, presented a 200 page report at a Tokyo news conference.

No skeleton has been found; only the skull. There is evidence of murder since a single bullet hole was found at the base of the skull. The report of the archaeologists and the mythology experts from Greece declares that the skull "will change the way we view the ancient myths forever. If Cyclopes existed, then there must be other aspects of the ancient myths that are true. The discovery of this skull puts us on the threshold of a whole new area of research."

It does indeed. The claims of the light seekers and the mystics have been somewhat vindicated—the claims that the gods and goddesses came to Earth in spaceships ages ago, and found Cyclopes, Titans and monsters already here. The recent finding of the Cyclopes' skull clearly reveals that the being did indeed exist. And if the Cyclopes, why not the Titans, the giants, and the gods?

The Titans

Like the Cyclopes, the Titans had among them both great benefactors and those who were destructive to Eartheans, who were then primitive cave dwellers. Mighty in strength, massive in size, the Titans were a formidable foe.

It should be understood that the Titans were themselves foreigners to Earth, travelers from some distant planet. They arrived on Earth prior to the arrival of the gods and goddesses who came to occupy Mt. Olympus. Therefore it is not surprising that conflict developed between these two great forces. Among the most renowned of the Titans were Atlas, Cronus, Prometheus, and their sister Rhea who was also wife to Cronus.

The Giants

The Giants were the brood of monstrous beings who were found to inhabit Earth when the gods arrived. They are described as an early race of mankind of exceptional strength and height, with frightening features, long beards and hair. It was they who warred against the Olympian gods and were only defeated because Hercules, a demigod, came to the aid of the gods.

Demigods

Among the gods and goddesses were many demigods and goddesses—those not having yet acquired the status of immortality. These were the "beautiful" of Earth, or the sons and daughters of a space god or goddess uniting with a "fair" Earthean. Among them were:

Asclepios, Atlas, Eros, Gaea, Cronus, the Muses, Oceanos, Agamemnon, Clytemnestra, Danae, Electra, Europa, Eurydice, Ganymede, Hector, Helen, Hercules, Hippolytus, Icarus, Jason, Leda, Leta, Medea, Menelaus, Minos, Odysseus, Oedipus, Orestes, Orpheus, Paris, Pasiphae, Penelope, Perseus, Pheadra, Phrixus, and Theseus.

Although this book is principally about the Mystery Schools of Greece, since the gods and goddesses of Mt. Olympus were involved in these ceremonies and initiations, it seems fitting that a sketch of each of the twelve be presented.

Chapter Three

The Gods and Goddesses

Zeus

Zeus

Zeus was the youngest son of Rhea and Cronus, who, in mythology, is called "Father Time." *Cronus,* king of the sidereal kingdom, was renowned for "devouring" all of his children to avoid the possibility of one of them eventually dethroning him— which means that *Time* always "devours" everything; everything and everyone succumbs to the passage of time. The myth states that *Rhea* took the last babe, a son, and hid him in a mountaintop cave in Crete, an island near Greece, so that Time (Cronus) could not "devour" him. She named him Zeus. He matured to take umbrage against Cronus, his father, to overcome him and to become the great Father-God and Creator of Greece—which means he learned the secret of physical immortality, the secret of overcoming time—and was not subject to death as we know it.

*Cronus was the youngest son of Uranus, the sky, and Gaea, Mother Earth. At the death of Uranus, he became ruler of the sidereal kingdom. Rhea, his sister, became his wife. They parented Zeus, Hades, Poseidon, Hera, Demeter and Hestia. So it is clear he did not actually "devour" his children. He symbolized **Time** in the world of matter. The devouring of his children means that no soul in the physical world escapes the ravages of time— not yet, anyway.*

Zeus reigned on Crete long before establishing Mount Olympus as the headquarters for the gods from outer space. Having arrived on Crete from some celestial star, he built magnificent *Knossos*, the incomparable palace and Mystery School of Crete. The ruins of Knossos have only recently been discovered, and are even now still being excavated from the debris which covered them following the devastating earthquake which demolished the islands of Thera and Crete in the middle of the 5th century B. C.

Zeus, along with other Greek gods, was endowed with the attributes of the solar deity, which again implies they came from outer space, possibly the sun itself. The Greeks not only recognized Zeus as the supreme leader of the solar energies, but attributed the same energies, with lesser quantities, to Apollo, Dionysus and Hermes. Actually most of the gods of antiquity were involved with the worship of the sun, were associated with God himself, and some were actually called sun gods.

The image of the sun god pictures a beautiful blue -eyed, beardless youth with golden hair falling loosely upon his shoulders. He appears to be androgynous, effeminate qualities balanced with masculine. He wears a spotless white robe which covers him from shoulder to foot. Many of his images depict him carrying in his arms a tiny white lamb, symbolic of the Lamb of God, also symbolic of the vernal equinox. This remark-

The Sun God and the Zodiacal Kingdom

able young god is a composite of Zeus, Apollo, Osiris, Orpheus, Dionysus, Hermes, and Mithras. Each of these pagan deities shared characteristics common to the solar deity. The light radiating from the youth, representative of the solar deity, extended to all parts of the celestial and material universe.

Even in the pagan Mysteries the 25th of December was recognized as the birthday of the solar god. Symbolic of the vernal
equinox, it heralded the return of light after the darkness of winter. The sun god was always reborn on that day, bringing life and
fertility again to the Northern Hemisphere.

In the Mysteries, Zeus was called the "immortal mortal." He
was also called "the ancient of days" and the "demiurgus." He
was a form of Jehovah, the creator of the Kabbalists. Zeus, god
of gods, son of Saturn-Time, had no beginning and no ending. He
was eternal. The Orphic Mysteries declared him to be the beginning, the middle and the end of all things. "Out of Zeus, all things
have been made." The Pleiades of Dodona said, "Zeus was, Zeus
is, Zeus will be. Oh, great Zeus." Homer made him the combined
attributes of God. He was called "the parent of instruction, the
school master of life." He concealed the element of fire. But his
total object was to improve life for Earth's mortals.

His principal activity was to select special Earth maidens with
whom to mate, to beget semi-gods and goddesses, to leave on
Earth a seed of his divinity in the bloodstream of special Eartheans. He left the formation and spread of the Mystery religion to
other gods and goddesses.

The greatest of all Greek sculptors, Pheidias, built on Mt.
Olympus a colossal statue of Zeus, god of the gods. The enormous statue was overlaid with ivory, the robes of molded gold.
In one hand the god held a globe upon which stood the goddess
of victory, Athena, his twin soul. In the other he held a scepter
topped with a flying eagle. On his head he wore a crown of olive
wreaths. The face was heavily bearded. The god was seated upon
an immense throne carved in elaborate symbols. He was every
inch a king and even more—an immortal god.

Painting by Charles M. Sheldon

Zeus

Pheidias' statue of Olympian Zeus, which is considered to be one of the Seven Wonders of the World.

Hera

Hera was the daughter of Cronus and Rhea, and sister of Zeus. She also became his second legal wife, the first being Metis. She was the epitome of perfect beauty. Being the goddess of marriage and of childbirth, Hera was venerated in every home. Yet with all this she seems to have spent a great share of her time pursuing vengeance upon any female goddess or mortal who was unfortunate enough to mate with Zeus, her husband. In spite of Hera, with his many feminine lovers Zeus begat Hercules, Hermes, Dionysus, Apollo and Artemis. Hera is also called Juno—the name having been given to her by the Romans.

Hera

She never seemed to forget the part that his offspring played in her husband's life and forgiveness came hard. It seems not to matter how reluctant were many of these feminine partners of Zeus, or how innocent, she still pursued her vengeance. With Zeus, she begat several of the gods of Olympus—Ares, Hebe and Hephaestos. Apparently both Zeus and Hera did not care for Ares who appeared to be too violent, hateful and ruthless. Hebe, their daughter, was the goddess of youth. Hephaestos was ugly and lame, although highly honored among mortals because he was peace-loving and kindly.

Pallas Athena

Pallas Athena (called Minerva by the Romans) was the daughter of Zeus and his first wife Metis. When Gaea prophesied that Metis would give birth to one who would dethrone Zeus, he promptly swallowed Metis, his twin soul, which means they simply merged as feminine-masculine counterparts, she to become an innate part of Zeus. Later, he suffered dreadful head pains. They were only relieved when Athena sprang from his opened head fully matured and fully armed. Known as the warrior goddess, and having sprung from the head of Zeus, we can interpret the legend to mean that Metis emerged from her soul-union with Zeus to reign as Athena, the feminine aspect of Zeus, equal to him in all things. She did not dethrone him but she matched him in many battles for good and for justice.

As her armor would indicate, Athena was a warlike goddess—Metis reborn—but she used her powers to defend the state and the home from outside enemies. She was sought through prayers, ceremonies, and sacrifices to protect agriculture and navigation—and also those commonly associated with the hearth, such as spinning, weaving, pottery and needlework. She was the goddess of the city of Athens, protectress of civilized life. She is credited with being the first to tame horses for mortals to use, and inventing the bridle.

She was Zeus' favorite "child." Again, she actually was not his daughter but his twin soul, being a reemergence of Metis, his feminine counterpart. He submitted to her representing him by trusting her to carry his full armor: his buckler and his devastating weapon, the thunderbolt. She was also recognized as the embodiment of wisdom, reason and purity. Being the feminine aspect and counterpart of Zeus, she was the most powerful of all the goddesses of Olympus.

Athena

*A reproduction of Pheidias' gold and ivory statue of Athena that
once stood in the Parthenon.*

Poseidon

When the gods first arrived on Earth, they divided the planet into territories, each god or goddess reigning as king or queen over a portion. Zeus reigned in heaven, or in etheric Mt. Olympus; Hades reigned in the netherworld; and *Poseidon* was made god of the seas. He was given the island continent of Atlantis to rule. His major weapon was called a trident, a three-pronged scepter capable of controlling the sea and earthquakes—obviously some type of advanced laser ray. Poseidon was recognized as the disobedient and rebellious god in that he constantly opposed the laws laid down by Zeus and the council on Olympus.

The island of Atlantis, his headquarters, was abundant with natural resources. Plato describes it as a paradise on Earth. On the island Poseidon met and married the beautiful maiden, *Cleito.* They begot five pairs of male children. Poseidon divided Atlantis among these ten, giving *Atlas,* the elder, leadership over the other nine. The descendants of Atlas were to continue as rulers of Atlantis.

Each established his own form of government, but they maintained a mutual relationship which was governed by a code created by all ten kings and carved into a column which stood in the midst of the temple of Poseidon. Every five or six years each of the ten kings made a pilgrimage to the temple of Poseidon so that they might renew their vows of loyalty to the code mutually established between them.

Poseidon—Ruler of Atlantis

Chief feature of the code was the oath that they would not ever take up arms against each other and that all would come to the aid of any of their number in times of attack. As the empire grew in power it was finally decided that the Atlantean kings would unite to conquer the entire world—at least the Grecian world. But Zeus, in Mount Olympus, through spiritual perception, discovered the wicked plot. He gathered around him all the gods and goddesses of Olympus, preparing a defense. Plato's narrative, *Critias*, ends just as Zeus is about to give directions to the Olympian gods. But the story is continued by Solon, Egyptian priest. Poseidon did attack Athens and was overcome by the goddess Athena. The battle caused violent earthquakes and floods which shook the Earth. So great was the catastrophe, Atlantis itself met its doom and sank beneath the waves of the Atlantic Ocean. The rains following the violence continued until a deluge ravaged most of the Earth.

(Extraterrestrials now visiting our planet tell of this horrible happening in greater detail, as they make contact with certain Earthean contactees. They tell us the Atlanteans perfected a deadly weapon with which they meant not only to conquer and dominate Earth but also other planets. But Zeus and the council at Mt. Olympus sought aid from beings on other planets who arrived on Earth to help the Olympian gods and goddesses subdue Poseidon and the Atlanteans.

Through their united efforts the monstrous weapon backfired, causing Atlantis to erupt in a gigantic destruction. The island sank beneath the seas, taking with it the enormous pyramid which had housed the weapon. There, in what we now call the Bermuda Triangle, the weapon is still active when the rays of the sun or certain stars strike it from a particular angle, causing the total disappearance of planes, ships, boats and people into or through a time warp or a dimension warp. These same ETs warn of a danger to us from this source and one of their present missions is to skillfully dismantle this awful weapon before its deadly rays can destroy Earth.)

To repeat, some believe the island of Thera—now called Santorini—may be a remnant of Atlantis. The Athenian writer, Solon, described his journey to Egypt where the scribes told him of the disappearance of Atlantis 13,000 years ago. The Egyptians described a lost land of Atlantis, an ancient island, vanishing in 24 hours under a tremendous tidal wave.

Whether or not Santorini (Thera) was part of the glorified Atlantis of the ancients is not known. But the ruins of Minoan life through volcanic explosion and subsequent tidal wave and earthquake, indicate it could be possible. In 1883, Krakatoa exploded creating a gigantic crater, which vacancy caused a tidal wave more than 660 feet high, spreading damage over 100 miles. Such a volcanic explosion certainly destroyed the civilizations of Thera and Crete. Whether or not they are remnants of the islands of Atlantis awaits further research. At any rate, with the destruction of Atlantis, the reign of Poseidon came to an end.

Artemis

Artemis—called Diana by the Romans—was the daughter of Zeus and Leto, and twin sister of Apollo. She was the goddess of fertility and the hunt. She was also the goddess of chastity. She was best loved by the Ephesians and the Cretans. We'll have more to say about her when we speak of the Mysteries of Ephesus.

Apollo

Apollo was the son of Zeus and Leto, a demi-goddess. She was the daughter of the Titans Coeus and Phoebe. To escape the wrath of Hera, Leto fled to the island of Delos where she gave birth to twins—Apollo and Artemis. There is no mistaking the godhood of Apollo, for no mere man of Earth could ever possess his many qualities of leadership, which matched those of the immortal Imhotep of Egypt, another space god. Apollo is renowned for the temple of Delphi. He was also identified with the sun as a sun god. He was called the god of archery, music, medicine and prophecy.

He was one of the most handsome of the gods—and certainly one of the most beneficent. Among his wives were Daphne, Clytia and Coronis, who bore him a son Asclepios. His weapon was the

Apollo

bow and arrow—which was, of course, a mighty laser ray weapon, not the bow and arrow of today. The rays of this powerful weapon, penetrating his enemy, brought instant death. Or with it, he could create plagues and famine.

He was, however, a god of love and light. He invented the lyre and his music was rivaled only by Orpheus, his son, with his magical lyre, which was given to Orpheus as a gift from Apollo. But he is best remembered as the god of prophecy, reigning as the overshadowing god at Delphi, the temple renowned universally for its unparalleled prophecies for hundreds of years. We shall have much more to say about Apollo when we teach of the Delphic Oracle.

Dionysus

Dionysus arrived late on the Mount of Olympus and became one of the twelve immortal gods only by replacing Hestia among the twelve in the hierarchy. He was the son of Zeus and the mortal *Semele*, daughter of Cadmus, of the house of Thebes. As the son of Zeus, Dionysus possessed the highest form of the fire of spirit. As the son of Semele, an Earthean, he had his roots on Earth—half-god, half-man. His semi-divine birth gave him access to heaven, to Earth and also to the underworld. All historical sources agree that Thebes was his birthplace.

The legend says that Zeus fell so madly in love with Semele that he swore to grant any wish she asked of him. She requested that she be allowed to see him in his full regalia and splendor as Lord of Olympus. But Zeus knew full well no mortal could behold him thusly and survive, and he realized his jealous wife Hera had put this thought into Semele's head knowing it meant her death. But he had sworn by the river Styx and such a vow must be honored. So he was forced to appear as a god. Beholding such blinding radiance electrocuted the form of Semele. But as Semele was dying, Zeus snatched from her their child that was near birth. He hid it in his own side out of Hera's sight until the time of birth. He named his new son Dionysus. Then he requested that Hermes take the babe to be raised by the nymphs of Nysa, the most magnificent of Earth's valleys. The nymphs were half sisters of the Pleiades. So grateful was Zeus he set the seven sisters among the stars.

When Dionysus grew to manhood, he wandered to many strange lands, teaching of initiation and the Mysteries. He came upon the island of Naxos and found Ariadne, princess of Crete, who was pining for Theseus, prince of Athens, who had deposited her there. He and Ariadne fell in love. Theseus, sad and despondent, sailed for Athens alone. Ariadne died and Dionysus took the crown he had given her and placed it among the stars. We'll speak more of Theseus and Ariadne later.

Dionysus

Dionysus longed for Semele, his dead mother. He sought her in the underworld and brought her back to the land of the living but decided she should live on Olympus. The gods accepted this unusual mortal because she had mothered so great a son.

He became known as the god of revelry through his connection with drinking ceremonial wine. His processions were known to be filled with drunkenness and revelry because of imbibing the wine presumably advocated by the god. But the purpose of the wine was only to liberate the worshipers from the restraints of self-consciousness and give them further access to cosmic awareness through a free-seeking consciousness. Delivered from the crystallized dogmas and doctrines of the current faith, the revelers imbibing the wine were supposed to use their freedom of restraint to become highly attuned to spiritual forces. We shall have much more to say about Dionysus and his "wine doctrine"— actually a Eucharist—as we move into the Mystery initiations.

Aphrodite

Aphrodite

Aphrodite—known by the Romans as Venus—was the goddess of love and feminine beauty. She "sprang from the sea," having neither father nor mother among gods nor mortals. This points to the certainty that she came Earthward from some distant star, that she arrived by a spaceship which could traverse the sea as well as the air, that the ship landed first in the sea from which she emerged as a divine goddess.

The ship which brought her landed in the waters near the island of Cyprus. She simply stepped out of the ship and the sea to join the Phoenicians as an aspect of Earth Mother Goddess. She held magical control over all the elements—the winds, the waters, the fires and the earth.

One of the most famous of the myths surrounding Aphrodite is that which concerned Paris, son of the King of Troy. The goddesses of Olympus decided to determine which of them was considered to be the most beautiful—these included Athena, Aphrodite and Hera. They appointed Paris to be the judge of this most unique beauty pageant. He chose Aphrodite and awarded her the prize, a golden apple, thus making enemies of the other two. She was called the "beautiful golden goddess" and no doubt deserved the apple.

She was supposedly wed to Hephaestos, god of fire, but her one true love was Adonis, who loved to hunt in the woodland ways. She often shared the chase with him. But one day during her absence, Adonis tracked down a treacherous boar. He hurled his spear but only succeeded in wounding the beast, who charged and gored him. Aphrodite, hearing his cries, fled to his side but could not save him. He died in her arms.

Ares

Ares was a very unpopular son of Zeus and Hera. As their son he occupied a place on Mt. Olympus, but in all his characteristics he represented all that is alien to the ideals of a god. He was ugly, violent and warlike. Both his parents disliked him. So did most of Greece because he took part in battles against mortals.

Hephaestos

Hephaestos was the son of Hera and Zeus. He was born ugly and lame. But because he was peace-loving and concerned with the welfare of Eartheans, he was greatly loved. He worked closely with Athena to oversee handicrafts and arts. He used his genius and skill to forge fine metalwork, such as the shields and armor of warriors and gods. The renowned shields of both Zeus and Athena are credited to the creativity of Hephaestos. Some say he was married to Aphrodite, but such a marriage is difficult to imagine—she with her remarkable beauty, passion and unruly behavior, and he with his handicaps. It seems more probable that he was wed to Aglaia, one of the three Graces.

The three Graces were Aglaia, Euphrosyne and Thalia, daughters of Zeus and Aphrodite. These three sisters were the epitome of poetry, beauty, music and the dance.

Bas-Relief, Rome

Hephaestos and the Cyclopes forging Achille's shield.

Demeter

Demeter was the daughter of Cronus and Rhea. She was the goddess of agriculture, especially of grains and fruits. It was she who presumably brought wheat to Earth from some distant planet, because of her unsurpassed compassion for mankind.

She is best known for her part in the Mystery of Eleusis and her association with her daughter *Persephone*, whom she begot with Zeus. Much more will be written about her as we move into the Eleusinian Mysteries.

Demeter

Hermes

One of the most illustrious gods arriving from outer space and sharing rulership on Mt. Olympus was *Hermes*. He was the son of Zeus and *Maia*. He was as famous in Egypt as he was in Greece. And the Hebrews knew him as *Enoch*. He was recognized by all as *the messenger of the gods*. He later became *Mercury* to the Romans. Among the gods of Mt. Olympus none attained the fame and stature of the god Hermes. He was called *Thoth-Hermes* in Egypt. He is often called "Thrice Greatest"—*Hermes-Trismegistus*— because he was considered the greatest of all philosophers, the greatest of all priests and the greatest of all kings.

It's beyond understanding how this great one vacillated between Greece and Egypt—not in a sense of indecision but because apparently both civilizations were going through their "miracles of evolution" simultaneously. This man of consummate wisdom—who was initiated in the Mysteries of India, Asia and Ethiopia—was called *Taaut* by the Phoenicians, *Hermes-Trismegistus* by the Greeks, *Adris* and *Enoch* by the Hebrews and *Thoth* by the Egyptians.

In Egypt, Thoth is shown as one of the most divine Ptahs in the Mystery Schools. In the Mystery initiations in the Great Pyramid he acted as the recorder during the weighing of the hearts of the dead in the Judgment Hall of Osiris.

Iamblichus, writing about the renowned god, proclaimed him the author of 20,000 books. Manetho increased it to more than 36,000. The books he wrote in Egypt were written upon papyrus. Such a library of learning would incline one to think that no one individual could have accomplished such an overwhelming feat—and that there would have been a succession of followers taking the name of the god and continuing his monumental labors. But this isn't necessarily true. If the gods of Olympus were immortal, they could

Hermes

have retained their physical forms for centuries, during which time Hermes could certainly have accomplished all the magnificent deeds attributed to his name. One of his greatest secret teachings concerned the regeneration of humanity and in this writing he described how it might be attained. The book truly offered the key to immortality.

Most of his writings have long since vanished, but we still have copies of *The Emerald Tablet* and *The Divine Pymander*. Nothing has ever surpassed his writings on *The Tablet of Emerald* which he brought with him on his spaceship. The words said, in part: *What is superior is as that which is inferior, and what is below is as that which is above, to form the marvels of the unity.* This expresses without equal the law of equilibrium and of correspondence—of man's identity with the Creator.

He was considered to be the god of wisdom and of letters. He not only wrote innumerable books and scripts, but he taught humans how to write, how to arrange their speech, how to institute ceremonies, how to interpret the course of the stars, how to write music and musical harmonies. He revealed information about medicine, the art of working in metals, the lyre with three strings, physical exercises, arithmetic and hieroglyphics.

In Egypt, he chose a select group of initiates capable of understanding somewhat of the Mysteries and called them "priests of the living god." Both Greeks and Egyptians considered him actually to be one of the "living gods" sent from God to reform men, to lead them from their vices and show them the pathway leading to immortality. He taught of one supreme God and of seven principal deities. Could these seven have later been called the seven Elohim?—the Christian "angels before the throne of God?"

It was Hermes who built the great temple of initiation standing in the midst of Egypt—the Great Pyramid. This marvelous structure served many purposes. First it served as an Ark of the Covenant, radiating beams of energy to guide spaceships arriving from distant planets. As such, it also acted as a center of communication, receiving and transmitting messages of the aliens who occupied many centers of light all over the planet. Next, the nuclear reactor in its capstone distributed rays of energy not only throughout Egypt but throughout distant lands. Its beams of energy connected with other points of communication throughout the planet, forming a gridwork of meridians worldwide. And last, it acted as a temple of initiation, being a major Mystery School of antiquity. It was not constructed as a tomb for any pharaoh or king.

Teaching the secrets of the Mysteries, Hermes communicated such secrets only to initiates, requesting of them a binding oath never to divulge the secrets except to those who, after long trials of purification and discipline, should be found worthy to receive them. In other words, he left in the hands of the priests the wisdom to select those who would become keepers of the secrets. Orpheus was one such seeker. So was Pythagoras.*

Among his most important writings were the Masonic Initiatory Rituals, almost all of the Masonic symbols being Hermetic in character. Albert Pike, renowned writer of Masonic as well as ancient Mysteries, called Hermes the "Word of God." He says that God "sent" Osiris, Isis and Thoth (Hermes) to Egypt to point mankind toward a sure pathway to His heart. The three established the Osirian Mysteries in Egypt, with Thoth-Hermes the teacher of priests and hierophants. He taught them the abstract sciences, enigmatic geometrical theorems, fine art and the methods of initiation. He taught the knowledge of the zodiac and the course of the planets. He appointed festivals for sacrifices to the sun at each of the zodiacal signs—but not blood sacrifices. Instead, he taught of sacrifice by abstaining from pleasure, fasting, prayer and tithing—a different kind of "human" sacrifice. In the Egyptian Mystery Schools he wore the mask of the Ibis.

---

*See *The Secret Wisdom of the Great Initiates* by Earlyne Chaney, available from your bookstore or Astara.

Hermes was one of the great philosophers of antiquity whose works, deeds and writings were not at first destroyed by the early Christian fathers. Even they bowed to his teachings with respect. However, most of the books authored by Hermes were finally destroyed during the burning of the Library of Alexandria in Egypt by Christian zealots. Much of the fury of the Christians, in carrying out such a deed, was to eliminate his books because they realized that so long as his writings were in existence the Egyptians could never be brought into subjection. Many of the volumes, however, were stealthily removed from the library and buried in the desert. Perhaps some day they will be found and lift us again to a higher understanding of truth and wisdom.

In the Mystery temples, the Book of Thoth was kept locked in a golden box in the Holy of Holies of the temple. Only the Ptah carried the key. He alone knew the secrets revealed in the book. Some say that the Book of Thoth and the secrets of immortality are hidden in an arcane fashion in the Tarot cards—a loose leaf card book with 78 cards.

Hermes-Thoth wearing the Ibis head as he appeared during initiations in the Mystery Schools. He is also wearing a winged globe and helmet headdress which suggests he communicated with the gods of the solar boats (spaceships) above Egypt.

The Egyptian priests reveal that at his death he said: "Hitherto I have lived an exile from my true country. Now I return hither. Do not weep for me. I return to that celestial country whither goes each in his turn. There is God. This life is but a death."

Mithras

Although Mithras was not an Olympian god, so great was his influence upon the ancient world, it seems fitting that a brief word be said about him. The enlightened mystic and teacher Zoroaster first brought Mithras, the Persian god, to mankind. Mithras was a sun god, which means that—like the other supreme sun gods of antiquity—Osiris, Hermes, Apollo—he was sent by our solar deity to manifest on Earth. His purpose was to aid in the evolution of the lifewave. This was the purpose of all the sun gods who became avatars, or light bringers.

Ancient man first sought to understand God through the establishment of nature gods, sun gods and astrology. By observing the heavens, the stars and, indeed, the universe, he hoped to further understand the function of God and universal law. He first learned to obey the Logos through such knowledge. The birth of the Mystery Schools on Earth involved an understanding of universal law as a part of the learning process called initiation.

Thus, early religions taught sun worship. They never once considered worshiping the sun as a center of energy. To them the sun represented the solar deity who had sacrificed his cosmic liberation in order to establish a solar system upon which a lifewave could evolve to the Godhead. Mithras, coming as a most powerful solar god, was accepted as an incomparable teacher. He quickly established the rites of the Mysteries in Germany, France and Britain, after first establishing a fountainhead in Persia.

His life compares astonishingly with the life of our own Jesus of Nazareth. He too was born inside a rock cavern at the time when the sun was in the sign of Capricorn. Only a few shepherds perceived his birth. His first food was the fruit of the fig tree. His clothing was made of fig leaves. One of his first tasks was to capture and kill the "sacred bull"—which actually is the bull constellation, Taurus, in the heavens. The cosmic symbolic "slaying" of this astrological bull released cosmic energies upon planet Earth which, again, were to aid the spiritual development of the lifewave and to usher in a new age.

The Mithraic rites of initiation bear a strong resemblance to present day Masonic rites. Like other Mystery initiations, the entire procedure was divided into seven stages. The highest could never be achieved until the neophyte had passed through all the preliminary degrees and was recognized as capable of proceeding. One of his/her initiations consisted of being thrust into a den with a savage beast. If s/he was successful in defending him/herself, s/he was permitted to progress to the next rite. S/he was never allowed to be slaughtered by the beast, but if it was realized that s/he could not defend him/herself and had to be removed from the den, s/he had failed his/her initiation. We are reminded of the biblical story of Daniel in the lion's den. It is not that the initiate sought to combat a lion with physical strength, but to subdue the animal through psychic means as did Daniel. Failure did not mean

Mithras slaying the astrological bull.

death, but simply that the initiate had not mastered the skill of subduing the animal through the powerful eye ray of cosmic intuition.

A higher rite awaited the successful initiate wherein he was exposed to the elements of storm, lightning and an unholy crash of thunder. Traveling through this exposure he was required to find his way to a safe haven, using only his intuitive knowledge of the heavens. In so doing he must swim a swift current, cross a parched desert, keep himself warm while trudging deep snows—he must prove himself master of the elements. Nor was exposure to the frozen snows an insurmountable task by an initiate who had evolved "Tummos" within himself, an inner fire which awakened during initiation, melted the snows, and created normal surroundings.

Daniel in the lion's den — aided by "Angels of the Lord,"
or space gods shielding him with their light rays

In his final rite he was led into a cave resplendent with an indescribable light. There he came face to face with the gods and goddesses of a higher world and was himself crowned as a god. So rigorous were the rites of the Mithraic Order no one sought entrance except the most serious and most capable. Initiates were given the names of the constellations. Their costumes and headdresses were representative of animals depicting the signs of the zodiac, even as did the ancient Egyptians. Their sacred rites included that of holy communion and baptism. Though many sought the Lesser Mysteries of Mithras, few ever emerged as fullfledged initiates of the Greater. "Many were called but few were chosen."

Chapter Four

Demigods, Titans and Heroes

Following sketches about the twelve gods and goddesses of Olympus, it seems fitting that we also speak of the demigods, the Titans and the heroes of Greece, whose destinies are interwoven with the gods and goddesses in the mysteries of antiquity.

Mycenae (Mi-se-ne), on the mainland of Greece, was a large palace dominating a surrounding area of limited population. The ruler over the palace, thus all the surrounding populace, was the Wadaca, the chief priest-king. He was not only the priest-king, he was ruler over the entire territory. As king, he was surrounded by a hierarchy of officials and minor lords who helped him carry out his innumerable and vast duties, supervising and directing the daily life of the populace. His officials, corresponding somewhat to a city council, also lived in the palace. Their task was to rule the territory. A class of scribes kept the records, including taxes and details of political events. The priesthood supervised the rituals of worship and issued prophecies. The Mycenaean culture, which dominated Greece, was at its zenith in 1500 B.C. No record of past history has ever been found in the ruins of Mycenae to disclose why this beautiful culture went into decline.

Perseus—Awakener of the Soul

The hero-founder of Mycenae was Perseus, son of the god
Zeus and the Earthean Danae. Danae was the daughter of Acrisius, king of Argos. With the birth of Perseus, King Acrisius set
both mother and son adrift at sea in a wooden ark. He did so
because he was aware of the cycle of fathers whose sons seized
power in the normal course of events. And he realized that, as the
son of Zeus, Perseus would display great power. Like the child
Moses, and the Egyptian Osiris, Danae and Perseus were saved
by King Polydeuces when their ark washed ashore at Seriphos.
Polydeuces promptly fell in love with Danae.

As Perseus matured, he became an obstacle in the love affair,
causing Polydeuces to persuade him to undertake a dangerous
venture—obtaining the head of the infamous Medusa whose face
turned all who looked upon it to stone. This was symbolic, of
course, of spiritual death or the temporary sleep of the soul.
Overshadowed by Hermes and Athena, Perseus was victorious
over Medusa. He battled her by viewing her only as a reflection
in his sacred shield, which symbolized seeing earthly life only as
a reflection of a greater reality, which allowed the soul to awaken
to its proper destiny.

Still under the guidance of Hermes and Athena, Perseus met
and fell in love with the beautiful Andromeda, became a king of
Tiryns and founded Mycenae with the help of the Cyclopes, who
constructed the huge walls surrounding the citadel, called the
Cyclopean Wall.

Atreus—Controller of the Elements

Then there is a story of how Atreus, as king of Mycenae, was
involved with the Golden Fleece. Atreus swore to the goddess
Artemis to sacrifice in her honor the finest sheep in his flock.
Knowing of this vow, Hermes planted a lamb with a golden fleece
among the herds to discover whether or not Atreus would keep

the lamb for himself. This act symbolized the temptation of a hero to claim for himself what rightfully belongs to the spiritual realm. Atreus kept part of his vow by sacrificing the meat of the lamb to Artemis, but he kept the Golden Fleece for himself.

Thyestes, his brother, continuously striving to dislodge Atreus from the throne, stole the Fleece. Possession of the Fleece, with its power to control rain, meant that whomever controlled the rain could assume kingship. Possessing the Golden Fleece gave Thyestes the right to challenge control of the kingdom. Atreus, to counter this action, reversed the movement of the sun so that it set in the east. Demonstrating such awesome control over the elements gave Atreus kingship again and his brother Thyestes was banished. The act of reversing the movement of the sun demonstrated Atreus' astronomical knowledge and power, thus establishing him as the rightful king of Mycenae.

Atreus then wed Aerope. They parented two sons— Agamemnon and Menelaus. Agamemnon became king of Mycenae and wed Clytemnestra who gave birth to four children—a son, Orestes, and three daughters, Electra, Iphigenia, and Chrysothemis. Menelaus became king of Sparta and husband of the beautiful Helen. In the meantime, the banished Thyestes fathered a son called Aegisthus. As evil as his father, Aegisthus later seduced Clytemnestra in order to gain rulership of Mycenae. This happened when Agamemnon went to Troy to fight the Trojan War.

The Trojan War was fought to rescue Helen, wife of Menelaus, who had been abducted by Paris and carried off to Troy. Agamemnon, as king of Mycenae, was chosen to lead the expedition to Troy to rescue Helen, a campaign which lasted ten years.

To prepare for victory, Agamemnon offered a sacrifice of his own daughter, Iphigenia, upon the altar of his own ambitions, which outraged his wife, Clytemnestra. He offered her as a sacrifice to the goddess Artemis, who bore anger against him for killing a hart in her sacred grove. Agamemnon knew Artemis could cause a calm on the seas which would detain the Greek ships when they set sail for Troy. But when Agamemnon sought to sacrifice Iphigenia, Artemis substituted a stag at the last minute. She saved Iphigenia and carried her off to Tauris to become her priestess.

Clytemnestra was so enraged that Agamemnon would consider sacrificing his own daughter, she persuaded the people of Mycenae to accept her assassination of Agamemnon when he returned from the Trojan War. Clytemnestra claimed her action of assassination as a rightful act of revenge, but this was not the true reason for her action. Actually, during Agamemnon's ten year absence she had fallen in love with Aegisthus, son of the banished Thyestes. Once Agamemnon returned home he fell victim to Clytemnestra's scheme to assassinate him. Orestes, son of Agamemnon and Clytemnestra, vigorously opposed the assassination of his father and barely escaped his mother's wrath by fleeing from Mycenae.

After Agamemnon's murder, Clytemnestra and Aegisthus ruled Mycenae, always with the realization that Orestes had escaped and would probably return someday to avenge Agamemnon's murder. Electra, another daughter of Clytemnestra, continuously cried out to the gods that justice be done. Eventually, Orestes did return, disguised and guided by Apollo who instructed him to kill his mother, Clytemnestra, to avenge the death of Agamemnon, his father. Orestes and Electra, brother and sister, lured their mother, Clytemnestra, away from the kingdom of Mycenae with the deception that Orestes had died. Thus confronting the disguised Orestes, Clytemnestra failed to recognize him. Once gaining access to Clytemnestra, Orestes struck her down. Then he also slew Aegisthus.

But rather than ascending the throne at Mycenae, Orestes was driven out by the avenging Furies, whose mission was to punish sinners. Orestes sought shelter at the temple of Apollo at Delphi. But the Furies continually assaulted him on a subconscious level, haunting him with guilt. Seeking to escape the guilt, Orestes traveled to Athens where he was brought to trial for the murder of his mother. There, the goddess Athena and the god Apollo absolved Orestes of his crime and cleared him of guilt. Athena was successful in breaking the cycle of death and vengeance. Thus ended the myth of Atreus, ending also the history of war, murder, and revenge which had been the basis of the House of Atreus and Mycenae.

Following the death of Agamemnon the Mycenaean citadel fell as a center of power. The entire myth and legend of Agamemnon and all that was involved speaks of the loneliness of humanity because of its severance from its gods.

Prometheus—Benefactor of Humankind

Prometheus was one of the most valiant of the Titans. Since he was a son of Iapetus and Clymene—who was the daughter of Oceanos, one of the greatest of the demigods—he was half-god, half-man. He possessed semi-powers of the gods, far above man, yet he could not attain to the full measure of the gods, such as immortality. He was caught in an unhappy circumstance—too human to dwell in Olympus with the gods, yet too godlike to find happiness among inferior human life on Earth. So he conceived the audacious idea of bringing heaven to Earth—of stealing the divine light and fire from the gods and bringing it to mankind. Each human was given a spark from the Eternal Divine Fire. But most were unable to sustain it in its full glory and used their portion for dark and evil purposes. Those who kept the spark alive attained a measure of godhood.

Great benefactor that he was, Prometheus gave mankind all manner of advantages which led them from a state of barbarism to civilization. He taught them astronomy—of the constellations, the mystery of the stars, the precise hour of rising stars, the zodiac. He gave them the science of numbers and the alphabet. He domesticated beasts to help them facilitate cultivation. He taught them of navigation and medicine. He shared with them the interpretation of dreams. He revealed the secrets of Earth in the mineral kingdom, including gold, silver, bronze and iron. He taught them all the mystical arts. But when he taught man how to harness electricity, Zeus rebelled.

Realizing that humanity was not yet evolved for such knowledge, Zeus launched a cataclysmic flood, not only to avenge Prometheus but because the race of Eartheans Prometheus had aided had grown wicked and sought to use electricity (lightning— divine fire) as a weapon of global destruction. But Prometheus, aware of the coming Flood, instructed his son Deucalion to build an ark and to take within it Deucalion's entire family. Thus when the Flood struck the Earth, Deucalion and Pyrrha his wife remained in the ark until it rested upon the peak of Mt. Parnassus. When Deucalion and Pyrrha emerged, they made a sacrifice to Zeus which greatly touched the god.

To further avenge Prometheus, Zeus sought Epimetheus, the brother of Prometheus, and offered him a gift—a lovely lady called Pandora. With her he gave a mysterious chest with a warning never to open it. Although Prometheus had warned Epimetheus never to accept a gift from Zeus, Epimetheus was so enthralled with Pandora's beauty he ignored Prometheus and accepted her with her box. Curiosity overcoming her, Pandora finally opened it—releasing upon mankind all manner of misfortune. Only one good thing was released from the chest, which was hope.

But Prometheus also brought mankind another kind of fire— that of evolved consciousness—a spark of divine fire to instill within the soul the opportunity for salvation or liberation from the wheel of rebirth. Zeus was angered because in the cosmic scheme of things the race was not yet prepared for such liberation. Zeus realized the soul of the lifewave must return again and again to the mortal realms until each soul became purified enough for the celestial realms of immortality.

When Prometheus revealed the secret of divine fire to mankind, Zeus, forgetting how Prometheus had come to his aid when the giants sought to destroy the gods, exacted a further terrible vengeance upon him by sentencing him to be chained to the topmost peak of the Caucasus mountain. Zeus had been proven right—mankind, with electricity and electromagnetism, had become extremely evil. So he chained Prometheus and sent a vulture to feed on his liver daily. The liver was restored each night. This torture continued for 30 years.

The Caucasus upon which Prometheus was chained rose high above the Earth—its summit so lofty that, like the Indian Mt. Meru, it connected both the upper and lower worlds. While

Prometheus was chained to the Caucasus, Hermes came to console him but, realizing the destiny of Prometheus, he said: *To such labors look thou for no termination until some god shall appear as a substitute in thy pains, and shall be willing to go both to gloomy Hades and to the murky depths around Tartarus.*

On such a pinnacle was Prometheus crucified until the mighty Hercules finally broke the chains to unbind him and slew the vulture to release him from his suffering—Hercules, the "only begotten one." It was Hercules who put an end to his torture by descending to gloomy Hades and by going around Tartarus. Zeus forgave Prometheus and finally welcomed him to Olympus. Prometheus, welcomed to Olympus as a god,

Prometheus and the vulture on Mt. Caucasus.

thus becomes one of the greatest martyrs for the benefit of humanity. He became the first friend of man to be crucified for the cause of human progress. He wears the label of the "first savior."

Having been welcomed into Olympus, perhaps the time will come when his benevolence again shines upon Earth—and Zeus, observing goodness as well as evil among mankind, might be willing for this fifth race to emerge into the Golden Age. Tartarus was described as the netherworld, thusly:

Bound in bitter chains beneath the wide-wayed
  Earth,
As far below the Earth as over Earth, is heaven
For even so far down lies Tartarus:
Nine days and nights would a bronze anvil fall
And on the tenth reach Earth from heaven.
 And then again falling nine days and nights,
Would come to Tartarus, the brazen fenced.

It was the mighty Hercules who made a descent into the hell regions, lower in vibration than Earth itself, in order to release his friend Prometheus. He went as a substitute for the pains of humanity, offering himself as a self-sacrifice.

Theseus—Slayer of the Minotaur

Legends concerning the Mystery Schools of Crete begin with a fair maiden named Europa who lived with her father, King Agador of Israel. The story begins with a dream Europa had. In the dream she saw two goddesses who told her that she was to be contacted by Zeus, who would plant his seed of divinity in her, just as Gabriel appeared to Mary to tell her the Holy Spirit would come upon her. This dream so frightened Europa, she departed her home to go with friends to visit nearby hills.

While there, she and the other maidens were busily picking flowers in a meadow. Suddenly the great god Zeus descended from Olympus in the form of a beautiful white bull. Europa was fascinated by the beauty of the bull and, following a hypnotic suggestion, climbed upon its back. Whereupon the bull quickly descended to the sea and swam to Crete, leaving Europa alone and frightened upon the shore. We realize this legend of Zeus as a white bull interprets to mean he appeared to Europa flying in a spaceship in the form of a bull to prevent frightening her. In this "animalistic" ship, he flew with her to Crete. After leaving her there on the shore, Zeus soon returned as a handsome stranger to wed Europa. He and the princess Europa parented three offspring—one a son named Minos, future king of Crete.

As a son of Zeus, Minos possessed extrasensory powers. Before he sought to claim the throne of Knossos, the enormous palace of initiation on Crete, he prayed to Poseidon to produce a sign that he had a just claim to the throne. Poseidon responded by sending a sacred white bull as a sign and asked that it be used as a suitable sacrifice to himself. Minos accepted the beautiful bull but was so enthralled by its beauty he decided to keep it rather than sacrifice it to Poseidon. This angered the god considerably, so that when Minos married the beautiful Pasiphae, Poseidon influenced Pasiphae to fall in love with the white bull. Pasiphae sought Athens' greatest artist, Daedalus, as to what could be done concerning her infatuation with the bull. Daedalus fashioned the likeness of a cow which mated with the bull in the name of Queen Pasiphae. From this union the Minotaur was born—half man and half bull. Minos confined the monster to the darkest recesses of the labyrinth beneath the palace of Knossos.

Now Theseus enters the story.

Theseus was the son of Aegeus, king of Athens. His mother Aethra was the daughter of King Pittheus of Troezene. When Aethra, the princess, became pregnant, she and Aegeus were not wed. Her pregnancy came about because when King Pittheus visited the Oracle of Delphi the Pythoness informed him his daughter Aethra would give birth to a remarkable child, fathered by a king. Immediately following this message, King Pittheus met King Aegeus, who was also seeking advice from the oracle. Disclosing the message to Aegeus, Pittheus persuaded Aegeus to mate with his daughter Aethra to produce this prophesied remarkable child. Aegeus agreed, fascinated by the possibility of fathering such a child.

When it was discovered that Aethra was with child, Aegeus took her to the palace of King Pittheus in Troezene to await birth of the prophesied child. Before he departed Troezene to return to Athens, Aegeus placed in a secret hollow a sword and a pair of sandals. They were covered with a great stone. He told Aethra that if the child was a boy, when he grew strong enough to roll away the stone and obtain the articles beneath it, he was to be sent to Athens bringing the sword and sandals with him, and Aegeus, recognizing the articles, would claim him as his son.

The child was a boy. He grew to magnificent manhood. When he had obtained maturity, his mother took him to the secreted hollow. There he lifted the stone with no difficulty, to obtain the sandals and the sword. She sent him to Athens, telling him he was the son of Aegeus, king of Athens. She told him his father would recognize him as his son upon seeing the sandals and the sword. His mother and grandfather, King Pittheus, supplied a beautiful sailing ship for his journey, but he steadfastly refused the use of it, declaring that this would be the safest way to journey. He considered the safest way cowardly, choosing instead to journey overland, which was fraught with danger, for bandits beset the road, often subjecting travelers to a most heinous death.

On his overland journey to Athens, Theseus slew the bandits, subjecting each of them to the same type of suffering they had dealt to others. He also slew the dreaded Boar of Calydon. After such feats of valor, his fame went before him. Upon arriving at Athens he was greeted by an enthusiastic populace, acknowledged as a great hero and invited to a banquet by King Aegeus to celebrate his deeds. Unaware that Theseus was his son, the king, fearing that the young hero had come to dethrone him, entertained the idea of poisoning him at the banquet.

The idea of poisoning came from Medea his wife, heroine of the quest of the Golden Fleece, who, through her sorcery, perceived the true identity of Theseus. As the queen, she feared his interference in her relationship and influence over Aegeus. But as she handed him the poisoned cup, Theseus, hoping to make himself recognized at once by his father, drew his sword. Aegeus instantly recognized it as the sword he had buried in the secret hollow and dashed the cup from Medea's hands. Medea escaped in her winged car and fled to Asia. Aegeus then acknowledged Theseus as his son and heir. As the heir apparent, Theseus took every opportunity to endear himself to the Athenians. He fought many battles and was recognized as a great hero.

Years before his arrival in Athens, a dreadful misfortune had befallen the city. Androgeus, son of King Minos of Crete, was visiting Aegeus, king of Athens. Aegeus had sent his royal guest on an expedition full of peril—to slay a dangerous bull. Instead the bull had slain Prince Androgeus. Distraught with grief, King Minos invaded Athens. With the city at his mercy he offered a stipulation: every nine years Athens would send him a tribute of seven maidens and seven youths to be sent to Crete. When they reached Crete they would be released into the labyrinth under his palace where no escape from the Minotaur was possible. Regardless of which direction they might run, eventually they would meet the Minotaur face to face to be slaughtered.

The time had come for the next installment of the tribute. Theseus, beloved by all for his goodness and nobility, immediately came forward, offering to become one of the seven male youths to be sent to Crete. He vowed to kill the Minotaur and abolish the tribute forever. Before departure, Theseus sought counsel at the Delphic Oracle, who advised that he should perform sacrifices to Aphrodite before embarking. Following this advice, Theseus then joined the other Athenian youths destined for death on the island of Crete.

When the unhappy ship set sail from Athens it carried a black sail. Aegeus had given Theseus a white one to be hoisted on the return voyage, as a sign to let Aegeus know he had been successful in slaughtering the Minotaur and was returning safely home.

On Crete, as the youths and maidens who were to die were paraded past the spectators in a public display before their slaughter, Ariadne, daughter of Minos and princess of Crete, fell madly in love with Theseus as he passed by her. Seeking him later, she offered him a magic sword with which to slay the Minotaur if he would promise to take her back to Athens and marry her. He immediately consented. Then she offered him a ball of thread which he was to unwind during his journey in the labyrinth. With these two weapons Theseus was victorious. With the magical sword he slew the Minotaur and, following the skein of thread, he found his way from the labyrinth. Then, taking Ariadne with them, the fourteen Athenians fled to the ship and escaped towards Athens.

They put in at the island of Naxos. There tragedy fell upon them. There are various reports of the tragedy. One declares that while Ariadne was asleep Theseus sailed away to Athens without her. The distraught Ariadne was found by Dionysus. The two of them promptly fell in love. Shortly afterward, Ariadne died.

Another version says that, since she was extremely seasick, the ship docked at Naxos to give her an opportunity to recover. While she was ashore, the ship of Theseus was blown out to sea because of a violent storm. While he was absent Dionysus found the beautiful princess, who, believing Theseus had perished in the storm, allowed herself to fall in love with Dionysus. The return of Theseus to Naxos was delayed a long time and when he returned, Ariadne had died. Because of the record of his past gallantry, this is probably the correct version.

In any case, grieving Theseus set sail for Athens, forgetting to hoist the white sail. His father, King Aegeus, seeing the black sail of his ship, assumed that Theseus had been slain by the Minotaur. Distraught, he leaped into the sea. After his tragic death, the sea was named after him, becoming the Aegean Sea. Theseus

Theseus slaying the Minotaur

then became king of Athens. As king, Theseus proclaimed special festivals to Dionysus to honor the memory of Ariadne.

Under his kingship he united the tribes of Attica to establish them as a great polis called Athens, after the goddess Athena, protectress of the city. He was one of the men who sailed on the Argo to find the Golden Fleece. His exploits of bravery and heroism continued to endear him to the Athenians to the very day of his death. His sanctuary can be found on the Acropolis, honoring him as the greatest hero of Athens. So beloved and so revered was he that there evolved a popular phrase, "Nothing without Theseus."

Asclepios—Genius of Healing

In Thessaly there lived a maiden named Coronis, so fair that Apollo fell in love with her. But before the child of their love could be born, Coronis fell in love with a mere mortal and was unfaithful to Apollo. When a white raven brought the sad news to Apollo, he became so enraged he turned the snow white raven's feathers black. Then, unwilling to destroy Coronis himself, he asked Artemis to slay her with one of her unerring arrows.

But so great was his grief at her loss, when he beheld the beautiful maiden on the funeral pyre as the flames leaped up around her, he snatched away the infant which was very near birth—just as Zeus had snatched the infant Dionysus when

Semele was near death. Apollo carried his infant son to Mount Pelion to leave him with Chiron, the wise and kindly Centaur who dwelt there in a cave. Apollo named the child Asclepios. Chiron had tutored the children of many notables—Achilles, Jason and Odysseus were his pupils—but this child was dearest of all to him.

He was not surprised when the young lad showed an intense interest in the art of healing and he shared all his secrets of the art with him. Chiron was a renowned master of herbs, poultices and potions. Nor was he surprised when his student surpassed him in healing powers and knowledge, since he was the son of a god.

The Centaur, half man and half animal, taught Asclepios all he knew of the spiritual sciences. The games, the music, the lectures, the drama, the purification, all were presented for the purpose of restoring health to the patients who sought healing. As a disciple of Chiron, Asclepios began his healing work with a blend of sacred science and secular medicine.

Asclepios became equally renowned, a universal benefactor. He even learned the secret of bringing the dead back to life. He thought "thoughts too great for man." Temples of healing in his name were created throughout Greece and Rome. Evidently Asclepios saw a definite connection between religion and healing for at one time there were over 300 temples attended by physician-priests where his methods were practiced. They were, in other words, health spas with strict rules to be observed.

Trikkla in Thessaly was the first place where Asclepios worshiped. Thessaly was known as the home of magic. Asclepios journeyed there to learn more of healing from the Thessalian seeresses—who were truly healers. They earned wide renown for cures they effected with herbs. Pythagoras is reputed to have visited Thessaly to learn from the Thessalian sorcerers how to hold a polished silver disk up to the moon to divine its message.

Magnets were a part of the healing shrines of Thessaly. A magnet was a part of the magic wand of Hermes. Asclepios also had a magic rod—the famous wand "through the possession of which a man becomes a master of healing." Homer, Pythagoras,

Epicurus and Aristotle were all familiar with the healing power of the magnet.

The secret about magnetism was kept from the uninitiated. Also, knowledge about the magnetic properties of amber. Pericles attributed much of his healing power to magnetism, laying the magnet in the center of the area of sickness. Later, laying on of hands took the place of magnets. Asclepios used magnets as an important part of his healing science.

A temple of Asclepios was also created on the island of Cos, which is the birth place of Hippocrates. The Asclepium on the island of Cos was probably the most renowned of his temples. It became one of the most sacred sites in Greece. Up to Roman times, people came from all over the world to be healed at its temple-hospital. Ptolemy the second was born there. Other healing temples were at Epidaurus, Athens, and Pergamos. A great springtime festival was celebrated every four years at all these temples. The greatest was at Epidaurus, which included games of athletic skill rivaling those of Olympia. Back of such activity was the purpose of healing, realigning the physical, psychic and spiritual energies of the body and soul.

Basically, his method of temple healing included four steps. First, each temple compound included water pools with healing herbs in which the patient bathed, cleansing the mind as well as the body—perhaps the first spa or jacuzzi. Diet was carefully supervised.

Second, after sundown there were rituals and various types of services to aid the patient who had psychic problems. This meant hypnosis, through which the patient recalled episodes in past lives which, remembered, cleared away the illness and phobias in the present life. These ceremonies also created oneness between the patient and the spiritual energies of the temple. Gems and precious stones were employed.

Third, the patient would then lie on a pallet of skins to fall asleep for the night in a chamber called the Abaton. This included incubation, a common medical term today. The patient was expected to dream and remember the dream's content. The dream frequently revealed the cause of the illness. Patients would describe their dreams to the priest-physician who would interpret them and prepare the proper medication. Fourth, sometimes Asclepios spoke directly to the patient during the dream, diagnosing and prescribing for the illness.

In the sanctuary of Asclepios, drama was presented as part of the healing process. To view the drama meant that the viewer was purged of thoughtforms which might have caused his or her illness or which may have prevented his healing. Asclepios worked more with the psyche than with the physical body, recognizing that mind played an important part in the healing process. In the dramatic presentations, the purpose was to align the viewer's body with that of Apollo. Asclepios worshiped Apollo, his father. He believed that worship of Apollo was the first step toward reestablishing balance in the body.

The dramas presented in the 15,000-seat stadium at Epidaurus created diversion for the sick visitors but at the same time stimulated the healing process through portraying the healing energies aroused by oneness with Apollo. Little remains of the temple today beyond the famous ruins of the two-story hospital. The theater at Epidaurus near Athens still remains one of the most incredible structures ever built. The dramas presented there were heard throughout the temple, the slightest sound on the stage, even a whisper, being discernible by those in the last rows of the theater. The temple, built in the forth century B.C. was certainly built according to the principles of sacred geometry.

Just outside the main temple stood a small temple dedicated to Aphrodite where the patient paused to make a sacrifice and pray for healing. The temple, 76 feet long and nearly 55 feet wide, housed an elaborate gold and ivory carving of Asclepios. In his right hand he held a healing staff and his left held firmly to the head of a serpent, which speaks loudly of his knowledge of the kundalini. It was his purpose in healing to arouse some measure of the kundalini force and bring it under control as the serpent in his left hand indicates. To achieve this purpose, Asclepios employed the use of music and other sounds and the force of light.

The inner temple was called the Tholos. The Tholos was built over a labyrinth of three concentric stone circles. This again speaks of secret ceremonies, welcoming the patient and the healed to initiation. In the Tholos were carved the names of renowned men and women cured by the god.

The labyrinth beneath the temple and the journey of the seeker through the stone passages clearly indicates the journey of the candidate during initiation. Perhaps the genius healer used initiation to restore the patient to health. Chanting, music and light involved in such a ceremony were obviously for the purpose of arousing the kundalini, which in turn restored the body to health. The labyrinth was a perfect circle. The entire structure of the Epidaurus symbolized the control of the spirit over the mind and the body. Its perfection spoke of perfect health and its inscriptions reminded the pilgrim that most of those entering its sacred walls regained physical, mental and spiritual well-being.

It was reported that among the healing techniques Chiron taught Asclepios was the usefulness of "a certain kind of snake," which was allowed to "lick" or touch the afflicted area, which brought about a cure. The snake was symbolic of rebirth and eternal life through cycles of regeneration.

This again would point to his knowledge of awakening kundalini, arousing its journey up the spinal column to touch the chakras on its way to the third eye in the brain.*

As the serpent kundalini wound its way up the spine, bringing about a healing, its completed journey to the third eye not only restored balance between the physical and spiritual forms but brought illumination to the one who was healed. After that, without question, the healed sought initiation which took him into the labyrinth below.

---

*See *Kundalini and the Third Eye,* by Earlyne Chaney and William Messick, available at your bookstore or Astara.

The name Asclepios has two meanings. One is "light" or a "mild radiance." The second is "earth," symbolized by the serpent. Even today the physician's symbol is the caduceus with two serpents entwined around a staff, symbolic of sushumna and raised kundalini. Asclepios also employed the use of surgical instruments and mixed his spiritual practices with standard medical practice.

Asclepios had two sons who became surgeons and helped spread his fame as a healer. However, they weren't nearly as well known as his four daughters—Hygeia, Panaceia, Iaso and Iagle—who also were healers in their father's temples. Hygeia, who offered principles and practices for preserving good health, is represented today in the science of hygienics. Panaceia's specialty was treating illness by means of herbs and other potions. Even today, the word panacea means a medicine which cures disease or any other kind of disharmony. Note that these two daughters are also included in the Hippocratic oath. Iaso must have been involved in healing through appealing to nature spirits or perhaps persons in higher dimensions. She is described as a healing

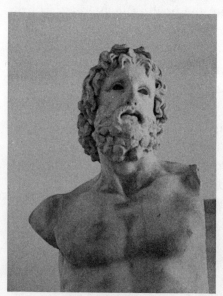

Asclepios

Nymph. Iagle, meaning "a being of light," used, under her father's guidance, shades and tones of light and color for healing purposes.

Asclepios was worshiped as a god, not only in Greece but in Egypt and Rome. Modern medicine still pays homage to him by requiring physicians to take the Hippocratic oath which begins with the words, *I swear by Apollo, physician, and Asclepios and Hygeia and Panaceia and all the gods and goddesses, making them my witnesses that I will fulfill, according to my ability and judgment, this oath and this covenant.* Then follows the regulations governing the physician's code of ethics and conduct. So the healing profession swore by the Olympian gods and goddesses, equating them with swearing in the name of God or on a sacred book, such as the Bible—and they still do today.

The death of Asclepios came about because, in his compassion as a healer, he restored a dead human being to life. This act angered Zeus, because to restore a mortal to life transgressed divine cosmic law. His reasoning was that it is not lawful to prolong life in the body when it is time for the soul to depart for the spiritual life. He struck down Asclepios with his lightning bolt. But he could not slay his fame. He was honored and loved as no other mortal. For hundreds of years following his death, he was deified. Patients prayed and sacrificed to him. He appeared in their dreams to prescribe cures. His temples remained sacred healing shrines.

Following the death of Asclepios, Apollo, his father, became so angry with Zeus he journeyed to Aetna where the Cyclopes forged the thunderbolts for Zeus, and slew them. Zeus in turn condemned Apollo to depart etheric Olympus and descend to Earth to serve Admetus, King of Thessaly, for a year.

Was Asclepios a figure of Greek mythology? A creation of classical poets? Or was he a person whose feats became mythologized? Was he a later incarnation of Imhotep, the Egyptian genius? His name is spelled several different ways. He's called Asklepios, Aesclepius, Esculapius—or Asclepios. Regardless of what name he was called, to the Greeks, and later to the Romans, he became the god of medicine.

Theseus and Ariadne

Chapter Five

Hercules—Demigod and Initiate

So great was Hercules and so renowned were his feats and his initiations, an entire chapter has been dedicated to this god-man. His entire life could be said to be an astonishing ongoing initiation.

Hercules was born in Thebes, the son of Zeus and Alcemene, who was a distant relative of Perseus. He too was part god, part man. He was also the object of Hera's wrath. At his birth she sent two dreadful serpents to strangle the newborn hero. But so great was his strength he crushed them both. Because of his immense strength and power even in childhood, he was sent to live on the mountains of Cithaeron where he grew to manhood. He became, without doubt, the greatest hero of the ancient world.

He married the princess Megara, daughter of the king of Thebes. It was Hera who sent a temporary madness upon him which caused him to kill Megara and their three small sons in a fit of anger. When the madness left him, he was consumed with grief and guilt to realize what he had done. His friend Theseus came to persuade him not to commit suicide but to go instead to Delphi and seek purification through the oracle of Apollo. It was Apollo, through the Pythia of Delphi, who bade him go to Eurystheus, king of Mycenae, and serve him as an act of repentance.

It was Eurystheus, under the urging of jealous Hera, who sentenced Hercules to the Twelve Labors for which he is renowned, each one of which were all but impossible. His First Labor was to kill the infamous enormous lion of Nemea, whom some say was the offspring of Typhon. Heretofore, all who had sought to slay the beast had met their deaths, regardless of what weapon was used.

Silver platter. Bibliothèque Nationale, Paris
Hercules and the Nemean Lion

Hercules found the lair of the lion on Mt. Tretus near Nemea, and saw the great lion returning from his daily kill. He shot a flight of arrows at it, but saw them fall harmlessly to the ground, unable to pierce the thick pelt. Approaching the beast, he next attacked it with his sword, but the sword bent as if made of tin. He next dispatched the ferocious killer with an untrimmed club cut from a wild olive tree. Then, seizing the stunned creature, he choked it to death. He carried the lion back to Mycenae. His garment from that time forward was often the lion skin. This First Labor initiates the passage of Hercules toward his ritual "death" in his initiation rites.

When he ventured upon his Second Labor, which was to kill the nine-headed Hydra of Lerna—a gigantic monster also born of Typhon—it was his niece Iolas who helped him. Hydra was an old serpent as large as a tree. Of her nine heads, eight were mortal and one was immortal. Dwelling on the banks of Lerna, she would often emerge from the lake, enter the neighborhood, and devour the living. With the aid of Iolas, Hercules finally destroyed the serpent. Iolas set one part of the surrounding grove afire, then, as

Hercules severed the mortal heads, Iolas burnt the stumps. Finally, using a golden sword, the immortal head was severed. One wonders if this "serpent" was not another "laser tank" similar to the "dragon" slain by Apollo on Mt. Parnassus at Delphi. The neophyte undergoing initiation must always battle the serpent, the bull, the lion, the boar or scorpion. These are all symbolic of the "phantoms on the threshold."

For his Third Labor, Eurystheus sent Hercules to capture a hind which was sacred to Artemis and bring her alive from Oenoe to Mycenae. The hind—with horns of gold and brazen hooves—dwelt in the forest of Cerynitia. Although he could easily have slain it, his orders were to take it alive, which required a whole year of his skill before he succeeded. Again, a hind "with horns of gold and brazen hooves" could have been a weapon brought to Earth from some other planet by the goddess Artemis—since there is no such animal on our Earth. As such a weapon, it must have been renowned for its ability to destroy, else Eurystheus would not have chosen it as a challenge.

Hercules chased the hind tirelessly, the hunt taking him as far as Istria and the Land of the Hyperboreans. There he caught her asleep under a tree and pinned her brazen hooves together. Slinging her across his shoulders he hastened through Arcadia to Mycenae, where he delivered her alive to Eurystheus. The chase of the hind symbolized the pursuit of Wisdom by the disciple on his/her initiatory journey. She is often to be found "reposing beneath the branches of the wild apple tree." Pursuing her a whole year and finding her near the Land of the Hyperboreans clearly indicates a gradual ascent towards final initiation. The wild apples symbolize treasures from the Tree of Knowledge.

His Fourth Labor was to capture alive the great boar of Mt. Erymanthus—a fierce immense beast which haunted the slopes of Mt. Erymanthus and ravaged the country around Psophis. To take such a beast alive was almost insurmountable, but Hercules accomplished it by driving it without stopping from one place to another until it fell in deep snow, exhausted. There, trapped,

Hercules bound it with chains and carried it alive to Eurystheus in Mycenae.

Boars were sacred to the Moon because of the crescent shape of their tusks. Hercules killing the boar in a snow drift mimics, in his initiatory rites, the Child Horus avenging the death of his father Osiris against his uncle Set who comes disguised as a boar. Slaying the boar indicates the victory of the disciple over the dark forces represented by Set.

The Fifth Labor was to clean the Augean Stables, which would have been a simple task except his orders were to accomplish it in a single day. The Augean cattle numbered in the thousands and their stables had not been cleared for many years. Hercules succeeded: first he breached the walls of the stockade in two places. Next, he diverted the courses of two rivers, causing them to flow through the stable in a great flood which carried away the debris within a day's time. One was the river Alpheus, the other Menius.

The cattle in this Labor are symbolic, hence their colors of red, black and white. The twelve sacred white bulls of the herds represented the twelve lunations of the Moon. The struggle of Hercules to turn the course of the river Alpheus represented the disciple overcoming a river god to successfully cleanse his bloodstream of the dung of picture images—or sins—which, flowing through the bloodstream, holds the disciple to his karma.*

His Sixth Labor was the killing of the infamous Stymphalian Birds which were fowls of vast dimensions. They had bronze beaks, claws and wings. Again, they would seem to be flying machines of some sort, since none of the feathered kingdom possess metal appendages. Infesting the marshes around Stymphalia in Arcadia, they devoured humans as their daily diet. They often swarmed up from the marshes in huge flocks, discharging a shower of brazen "feathers" which not only killed both man and beast, but blighted all the crops. It was Hercules who finally shot the birds with his arrows—his ray gun?—after arousing them

*See Astara's *Book of Life*, the hidden teachings of the degrees available only to Astarians. For information write Astara, 800 W. Arrow Hwy., Upland, CA 91786.

from their hiding place with a "brass rattle," which Athena had given him as a gift. What could possibly have constituted a "brass rattle" to cause the "birds" to attack? This Labor marks the disciple as achieving great success as a healer who can expel fever demons, which were always identified with marsh birds.

The Seventh Labor was to slay the beautiful white bull of Crete which Poseidon had given to Minos. This is not the Minotaur of Cretan fame. Minos offered help to Hercules, who refused it, though the bull was known to belch scorching flames (a flame throwing machine?). Hercules captured the savage beast and carried him alive in a boat to Eurystheus who, dedicating it to Hera, set it free.

The combat of the disciple with a man wearing the mask of a bull was one of the ritual tasks required for attaining initiation. It was a coronation rite where the horns of the bull, broken off as cornucopia in the struggle, were used to form a crown for the victorious initiate. The horns worn in the crown symbolized his attachment to the Moon goddess, the horns representing the crescent moon and the fruits of the cornucopia. Horns, through the ages, have been worn in

helmets and head-dresses by saints, warriors and initiates to designate supremacy, linkage to a Moon goddess or high initiation. The Virgin Mary is often depicted as standing astride a crescent moon which establishes her as a Moon goddess.

Hercules and the Stallions

The Eighth Labor was to slay the man-eating horses of King Diomedes of Thrace. Arriving at Tirida, Hercules was first challenged by the grooms who attended the savage stallions. He slew all the grooms. Then he drove the wild horses to the sea, leaving them on a high knoll. He then dug a channel which diverted sea water to flow into the lowlands of King Diomedes. Next he stunned Diomedes with his club and dragged his body, still living, into the pathway of the stallions, which he released from the knoll. He then harnessed the stallions to Diomedes' chariot and drove them back to Mycenae, where Eurystheus sent them to Mt. Olympus to be tamed by the gods.

The bridling of a wild horse was, again, a coronation rite. The initiate, entering a dream state (trance), was directed to mount the magnificent Winged Pegasus and soar aloft—in an out-of-body experience—to visit high astral realms and view their glories.

The Ninth Labor was to bring Admete, daughter of Eurystheus, the golden Girdle of Ares worn by Hippolyta, queen of the Amazons. Hercules set sail for the river Thermodon, which would carry him to the island of the Amazons. These mammoth women warriors carried brazen bows and shields in the form of a half moon. Their garments, girdles and helmets were made from the skin of wild beasts whom they had conquered. The Amazons were famed for having established several cities, one of which was Ephesus, where the magnificent Temple to Artemis was raised, rivaling the glory of Delphi.

Arriving at the mouth of the river Thermodon, Hippolyta met Hercules and, surprisingly, offered to give him the golden girdle as a love gift and would have done so had not Hera, still seeking vengeance, stirred within the consciousness of the Amazons the idea that Hercules had come to kidnap their queen. Believing this, the Amazons charged Hercules and his ship, whereupon Hercules was forced to slay Hippolyta and sail away with the girdle. Returning to Mycenae, he presented the girdle to Eurystheus who, in turn, gave it to Admete.

The capture of the golden girdle implies that the initiate took the vow of total chastity, represented by the girdle, or the vow of partial abstinence on the part of married initiates—thus to save the sexual energies to transmute them toward opening the third eye.

His Tenth Labor was to capture the Oxen of Geryon from the island of Erytheia and return with them to Mycenae without either demand or payment. Geryon was a monster with three bodies reputed to be the strongest man alive. The cattle, of marvelous beauty, were guarded by the herdsman Eurytion, son of Ares, and by Orthrus, a fierce two-headed watchdog. On his journey, Hercules, arriving at the land at the end of the Mediterranean, set up two great rocks as a memorial of his journeys. He called them *the pillars of Hercules*, which are now Gibraltar and Ceuta.

After a perilous journey, he arrived at Erytheia and ascended Mt. Abas. There Orthrus attacked him but Hercules felled him with his club, killing him instantly. Eurytion, rushing to aid Orthrus, met the same fate. Then Geryon himself challenged Hercules, but Hercules ran to Geryon's flank and shot him sideways through all three bodies with a single arrow. Thus he won the beautiful cattle without demand or payment. His return to Greece with the cattle was a long and arduous journey but he eventually arrived victorious.

The Eleventh Labor—the most difficult so far—was to bring back the Golden Apples of the Hesperides and present them to Eurystheus. The golden apple tree was Mother Earth's wedding gift to Hera, planted in a garden on the slopes of Mt. Atlas in the Land of the Hyperboreans. The Hesperides were the three daughters of Atlas, the powerful Titan whose duty was to hold the sky on his shoulders. Hera had given the Hesperides charge over the precious fruit of the tree, the Golden Apples.

The task was difficult because Hercules had no idea where the garden was to be found. He sought the help of Atlas, the father of the Hesperides, and asked him to obtain the apples for him, offering to take upon himself the burden of holding up the sky while Atlas accomplished the task. Atlas gladly agreed. Returning with the apples, he refused to give them to Hercules. Having secured Hercules to hold up the sky, he meant to keep him chained to the task, so that he might take the apples to Eurystheus himself. Hercules, finding himself burdened with the exhausting task of supporting the sky, agreed to the plan but asked Atlas to resume the duty momentarily so that Hercules might pad his shoulders to ease the pressure. Atlas, having again assumed the burden of the vault of heaven, Hercules immediately departed with the apples.

This myth covers the ritual of the initiate in conquering the science of astronomy and learning the secrets of the stars. When Atlas is said to "hold up the sky" it means that he was the first and most learned astronomer. He knew so much he carried the celestial globe "upon his shoulders." When Hercules took the globe from him, it symbolized the task of the initiate to learn the science of the heavens. Hercules, learning the science, became Lord of the Zodiac.

The Twelfth Labor was the greatest of all. He was forced to descend to Tartarus, the lower world, to capture the three-headed dog, Cerberus, bring him up from Hades and offer him to Eurystheus. To prepare for this task, Hercules went first to Eleusis, where he sought and received initiation into the Mysteries.

Cerberus was an enormous dog, possessing three heads. His neck was covered with serpents. His teeth were as venomous as a viper's. Stationed in a cave on the banks of the river Styx, he was the guardian of the netherworld. As guardian, he allowed the dead to enter the netherworld, but he barred them from ever leaving. Living mortals who dared approach his domain were torn to pieces by his three heads. There were those who could charm him, however, and obtain passage and return again to the upper world. One was Psyche, who was sent by Aphrodite to Persephone. She succeeded in passing him by feeding him a sweet. Orpheus charmed him with his lyre.

Hercules had only his strength with which to combat him. He had first to meet Hades, the king of the underworld. Hades consented to the capture of Cerberus only if Hercules agreed to use no weapons, only his hands. Even so, the strength of his hands overcame the terrible monster.

Once Cerberus was subdued, Hercules released Theseus from the chair of forgetfulness where Hades had imprisoned him in Tartarus when he had tried to help his friend Pirithos abduct Persephone for himself. In company with Pirithos, Theseus had descended to Tartarus to help with the abduction. But perceptive Hades, husband of Persephone, had become aware of their plot. He had bound both Pirithos and Theseus to certain magical chairs from which they could not release themselves. There they were doomed to spend the rest of their lives for punishment. When Hercules, returning with Cerberus to the upperworld, beheld both Pirithos and Theseus bound to their chairs, he released Theseus but was forced to leave Pirithos behind. Upon being released, Theseus was freed to the upper world and returned to Athens.

Hercules, in turn, lifted the three-headed, half-strangled Cerberus, carried him all the way to the upper world, journeyed with him to Mycenae and presented him to Eurystheus. Eurystheus, surprised that Hercules had accomplished the task, rejected Cerberus and insisted that Hercules return with him to the underworld. Returning Cerberus completed his last Labor. Only with the completion of these Twelve Labors did Hercules feel expiated from the awful slaughter of his wife and children. Although not compelled to do so, the heroic deeds of Hercules continued.

During these Labors, Hercules was required to journey all over the world, where he met other heroes, such as Theseus. It was on his way to obtain the Golden Apples of the Hesperides that he came upon Prometheus chained on the peak of the Caucasus, slew the vulture and freed Prometheus.

He also joined the Argonauts on their journey to capture the Golden Fleece. But he departed the ship, seeking his dearest companion, Hylas, who was lost. Hylas, the armor bearer of Hercules, left the Argos to draw water. As he dipped his pitcher into a spring a water nymph, observing his youth and beauty, drew him into the depths of the spring and he was heard from no more. Because he was very dear to Hercules, he departed the Argos in search of Hylas and did not return. Finally the Argos sailed without Hercules.

His deeds are almost too numerous to count. There is the story of Alcestis, daughter of King Peleus. Known for her great beauty, she had many suitors. To discourage undesirable suitors, King Peleus, with the help of Apollo, succeeded in yoking to his chariot a lion and a wild boar. The suitor successful in taming these beasts was considered worthy of marrying his daughter. She married Admetus, king of Pherae. But Admetus died from the bites of a serpent. Alcestis offered herself to go to Hades in his place, which she did. But Hercules, who wrestled with Death, rescued her from the underworld and returned her to Admetus.

He aided Zeus in his battle against the giants. The battle of the gods with the giants went through many stages. On the side of the gods were Zeus and Athena in the forefront. The second lineup included Hera, Apollo, Hephaestos, Artemis, Poseidon, Aphrodite, the Fates, and Hermes. Third in line was Dionysus. These few immortals faced the Titan giants who numbered about a hundred, thirty-four of whom were renowned for their gigantic size and heroism. The battle was desperate and uneven.

The Titan giants had advanced to the foothills of Olympus where the gods, being greatly outnumbered, were fighting a losing battle. Only when Zeus appealed to Hercules, one of the Titans, for help did the battle turn favorable to the gods. Hercules and Aphrodite concocted a scheme to hide him in a cave and she, with her womanly charms, would lure each giant to the cave where one by one Hercules slew them. Because of the help given by Hercules, the gods eventually triumphed, destroying all the giants.

No hero was as great as Hercules who embodied every aspect of superman, struggling with the forces of nature on behalf of humankind. Hercules was not only the strongest man on Earth, but, because he was the son of Zeus, he exhibited great beauty, courage and compassion. He constantly exhibited the most perfect confidence, realizing that he was part man, part god. He also often exhibited far more strength and courage than intellect. No physical force could overcome him. He could only be subdued by a supernatural force, which is what eventually brought about his death.

The legend of his death is itself immortal. When he had completed his Twelve Labors, he met and fell in love with Iole, daughter of King Eurytus. But Eurytus refused to give her as wife. For revenge, Hercules slew the king's son Iphitus. Realizing he could never have Iole, Hercules met, loved and married Deianira. Deianira sought the centaur Nessus as a teacher. During their friendship, Nessus gave Deianira a vial of poisonous vapors, telling her it was a love charm, and advised her to use it on Hercules were he ever to love another woman. When Nessus sought to violate Deianira, Hercules slew him.

Fulfilling his vow to some day punish King Eurytus for refusing to give Iole for his bride, Hercules collected an army, captured the king's city, and slew him. In so doing, he indirectly caused his own death. When securing the city, he captured a band of maidens and sent them home to serve Deianira. One of the maidens was Iole, the king's daughter, whom Hercules had loved. The man who delivered the captive maidens to Deianira told her that Hercules had again fallen madly in love with Iole.

Deianira—believing the report and hoping to regain Hercules' love—remembered the vial and, believing it to be a powerful love charm which would restore to her the love of Hercules, decided to use the vial. She sprinkled the poisonous fluid upon a splendid robe and had it delivered to Hercules by a messenger, requesting that he don it immediately. As he did so he was seized with a fearful pain, similar to a burning fire. In his agony, he had his soldiers bring him home to Deianira to die. But Deianira, learning what her gift had done, had, in her anguish, killed herself.

Upon learning of the death of Deianira, Hercules ordered his soldiers to take him to the peak of Mt. Oeta in the northern Land of the Hyperboreans where they built a great funeral pyre. Lying down upon it, he asked his youthful soldier Philoctetes to hold a torch to it and set the pyre ablaze. He gave him his bow and arrows. As the flames encircled his body, Zeus came to rescue and carry him to Olympus. There he was reconciled to Hera and married her daughter Hebe. He had finally attained his deserved rest in the home of the immortals on Olympus.

But the mighty Hercules was involved with more than one initiation into the Mysteries. In the land of Tyrc and in the city of Tsur the people celebrated a yearly festival of Mal-karth, the sun god, which was the incarnation of the sun at the winter solstice, or the return of the sun at the time of the winter solstice into the Northern Hemisphere, restoring life to the people. The celebration constituted the use of a pyre through which the god Mal-Karth, in the midst of the fire, might obtain a new life. The festival was celebrated on a day which corresponded to the 25th of December.

On one special year Khur-um, king of Tyre, performed this ceremony, and the god who was placed on the fire to obtain re-birth and awakening was Hercules, who experienced "death and resurrection" through this initiation by fire. We know, of course, that the fire was only symbolic, representing the divine fire, the White Light, of the resurrected or awakened soul, and that Hercules, as a son of Zeus, did experience initiation into the early Mysteries. In the Mysteries, too, the "fiery" death of Hercules was symbolic of the Phoenix process of perpetual regeneration, through which the spirit of the sun god lives on forever. The Phoenix is the mysterious bird who seeks its own death on a fiery pyre only to rise again from its own ashes, as did Hercules on the death pyre.

The journey of the sun through the twelve signs of the zodiac came to be called the Twelve Labors of Hercules. From this legend also came that of the murder of Khur-um, representative of the sun, later called Hiram, the immortal Master Mason. Hiram's murderers were the three ruffians of Masonry, symbolic of the three winter signs, Capricornus, Aquarius and Pisces who, assailing him at the three gates of heaven, slew him at the winter solstice and buried the great Master in a secret burial place. After the murder of Hiram, the nine fellow craftsmen of the Masons go in search of him and, finding his place of burial, resurrect him.

The First Labor of Hercules—his combat with the Nemean Lion—was the first sign into which the sun passed after falling below the summer solstice. Struggling to reascend, Hercules, as the sun god, eventually achieves his goal. Hercules, like all sun gods, is victorious over the great Typhon—the monstrous serpent of evil. All great initiates must meet and vanquish a serpent—or bring to full activity the awakened serpent fire of the kundalini. Krishna crushes the head of the serpent Calyia. Apollo slays Python on the crags of Mt. Parnassus. Hercules crushes the nine-headed Hydra, the serpent whose poison festered in the foot of Philoctetes. As an infant he also destroys the snakes sent by Hera to slay him. St. George of England and Michael the Archangel slay the dragon of darkness.

Herodotus, the ancient historian, declares that the name of Hercules was familiar in Egypt and the East long before he became a hero to the Greeks. The name of Hercules originally belonged to a much higher personage than the Greek hero. There still exists, according to Herodotus, the temple of Hercules in Tyre, built around 2300 years before the time of Herodotus. He declares Hercules to have been a hero of Phoenicia and worshiped as a sun god in the early Mystery Schools of that land. The victories of Hercules accentuate solar power, which is daily replenished, like the rebirth of the Phoenix.

The mountain he chose for his final fiery pyre lay in the far north among the mysterious Hyperboreans. On one of his journeys there he returned bearing the olive to the Greeks, after which the olive tree became sacred to the populace.

Master Masons declared the sun, as he traveled through the "living creatures of the zodiac," assumed the nature of triumph over each sign he entered. Thus the sun became a bull in Taurus and was worshiped as Apis and the god Serapis by the Egyptians. The Assyrians called the sun *Del Vaalbul.* In the sign of Leo, the sun became the lion slayer, Hercules. In the sign of Sagittarius the sun became the Archer. In Pisces he was Degon, our vision of the fish god. In Aquarius he becomes the solar man—or the god—who pours out new life upon humanity.

Albert Pike, master of Masonry, states that Hercules obtained his initiation from Triptolemus and became a living example of the teacher of the Mysteries. His vast travels, his heroic deeds, were the journeys of the initiate undergoing cosmic initiations. In Tyre, the titular god was styled Mal-karth or Baal, lord of the city. Her-culeus thus is a translation of Mal-karth and is Sanskrit in origin.

In writing his drama called *The Descent Into Hell by Hercules*, Aristophanes describes Hercules as an initiate descending into the realms of darkness for three days as do all candidates undergoing initiation. He has Hercules carrying lighted torches, symbolic of new life and resurrection from darkness. He has him undergoing a symbolic death and resurrection into light, representing eternal life. In such an initiation he also symbolized the sun god. Jesus "descended into hell" and ascended again after three days. So did Dionysus, Orpheus and Asclepios—all initiates "going to gloomy Hades and the murky depths around Tartarus."

It was Hercules, the initiate, during his travels throughout the nations, who became the adversary of human sacrifices and slew the men and monsters who offered them. He taught instead the offering of the divine fire without an obvious object of sacrifice, teaching that the fire of consciousness should be offered through prayer to the heavenly Father/Mother God.

Chapter Six

The Oracle at Delphi

As far back as time can be remembered, religion to the Greeks included worshiping nature spirits, the devas—the spirits that dwelt in the trees, the mountain tops, the rivers and in caves. In ancient Greece, long before the Christian era, many of these sites became sacred as oracles.

This came about because the land we now call Greece was endowed with electromagnetic gridpoints or Earth nodes that allowed the veil between this world and the next to be penetrated by spirit. These nodes were central points of concentrated pranic forces. Higher beings from the other side could more easily make contact at these gridpoints; could communicate and make prophecies and revelations. Many of these nodes were special caves around and over which the Mystery temples of initiation were constructed. Spirit teachers also used statues and psychics, as well as gems and certain precious stones through which to speak, to teach, to prophesy, to heal—such as the god who spoke and taught through Socrates, which Christianity later labeled his daemon.

Not only was the land itself subject to spiritual penetration but, because the race at that time was so involved with the worship of natural phenomena, humans felt themselves subject to control by natural forces. They sincerely believed they could abort cosmic dangers brought on by nature by supplicating the devas of nature. They were also fascinated with prophecies which might reveal approaching dangers or beneficent events. Becoming aware, through prophecy, of approaching natural dangers or catastrophes, they sought to offset such calamities by prayer, sacrifice and other supplications. They sincerely believed that with prophetic knowledge of beneficent events they might create festivals to pay homage to whatever forces were causative.

They came to take for granted knowledge of the future through the sites of prophecy—the principal one being the Oracle of Delphi. Many of the questions asked of the Pythoness—the Oracle—concerned the coming of good or dangerous events sent either through the wrath or benevolence of the devas and even of the gods. An oracle was, and still is, an especially ordained or divined priest or priestess who acted as a channel through whom the gods could communicate with those on Earth. The word *oracle* is derived from the Latin word *oraculum*, through the verb *orare,* meaning *to speak.* "Speaking" referred to messages of the gods given to seekers through priests or priestesses.

The Christian Bible is replete with prophecies given through prophets who were the same as the Greek oracles. Prophets were the instruments and channels of evolved spiritual teachers prophesying and guiding mankind through "prophecies." Prophets and oracles have existed since mankind first became thinking entities on the planet. Ancient writers through centuries of time have preserved for us authentic records of the prophetic knowledge of seers, prophets, priests, priestesses and oracles.

Certainly, the most famous of all sites for prophecies and messages for spiritual guidance was the Temple of Apollo at Delphi. It sat like a glowing gem of the gods on a plateau below the lower slopes of Mount Parnassus, whose peaks rise to an awesome height of 8,070 feet. The magnificent temple was wedged between twin limestone cliffs, each a thousand feet high, known as the Phaedriades—the Shining Crags. They were so called because when the light of the sun struck them at dawn they came alive with a radiant glow. The very choice of the site indicates the overshadowing presence and influence of a god. Only a god could have foreseen so awesome and soul-stirring a site and have executed its construction and its enduring activities—for many centuries, from 700 B.C. to 300 A.D.

Delphi was a natural setting for contact between spirit forces and Earth. The same is true of Stonehenge, Palanque, Machu Picchu, and other mysterious monuments, built on Earth grid-points to enhance the likelihood of spiritual contact. Before the enormous Delphic Temple became renowned for prophecies, the node was the location of a special megaron or ancient chapel where the Earth Mother Goddess held sway and initiations were performed. Sacrificial pits are still found. All these common areas of worship indicate a continuous history of religious activities at very special places. The early gods were well aware of the importance of certain sites for establishing their temples as a method of contacting spirits. The temples were not only built on electromagnetic nodes but the temples themselves were actually structured according to cosmic proportions through which to invoke the presence of the gods.

Long before time was recorded, the original site of Delphi was selected by spiritual guidance. Zeus, Apollo's father, released two eagles, charging them to locate the exact center of the world. They met at the center now called the Temple of Delphi, establishing it as an extremely potent gridpoint for miraculous forces, marking Delphi as the earth's navel or, as we would state it, the navel chakra or central point of the planet. The Greeks believed Delphi to be the umbilical point of the earth, the place from whence a mysterious etheric cord rose to ascend into celestial spheres, linking this node to akashic forces from higher dimensions.

A cone-shaped sacred stone known as the Omphalos was placed at the cave's entrance. An Omphalos stone, bound with fillets, was placed at the entrance of several temples of initiation. There was one at Eleusis and another at Ephesus. Each Omphalos emitted a special tone, a sound, which set into motion the etheric forces of that particular temple. The sound or tonal quality of each stone was different, and each tone emitted a different color, so that together the combined temples formed a cosmic rainbow. Each temple of initiation was linked with others through etheric streams of pranic force we now call *ley lines*. Together with their sounds and colors they formed a spiritual gridwork of the planet.

Many of the secret manifestations of the Mysteries could not truly have been understood by the profane, nor was the uninitiated populace capable of understanding the initiations. Certainly the Delphic Cave was sacred long before the time of the Delphic Oracles. It was an important force center of the Earth grid as far back as the Hyperborean age, which goes back as far as recorded history. Since the Delphic Cave came to be recognized as the navel chakra of the planet, we know that the ancients considered the planet to be an immense living entity.

According to Flavius Philostratis, the first temple at Delphi was formed only of olive branches and boughs from Apollo's sacred tree, the laurel. The second was similar except it was circled with stones, built by Trophonius and Agamedes of Athens. After this was destroyed by fire in

Omphalos of Delphi as it appeared in "olden" days.

548 B.C., a third was constructed, and brass replaced the stones; the fourth of marble and of great symmetry. The fifth became the awesome cave-temple of unmatched majesty we see and hear about today, erected between 530 and 514 B.C. by Spintharus of Corinth.

For us to understand the Mysteries of Delphi we must first know the story and the mysteries concerning Apollo, because the Oracles of Delphi were established through the overshadowing influence of the "resurrected" god.

Apollo was one of the twelve gods occupying the golden Mount of Olympus. He was the son of Zeus and Leto and the twin brother of Artemis. Most assuredly he was a god. Apollo is renowned as the spiritual force overshadowing the Temple of Delphi. No other oracle in Greece ever equaled the splendor of Delphi at its zenith. It contained innumerable statues of solid gold and silver and unnumbered works of art and beauty, donated by kings, princes, world leaders, who journeyed from all parts of the civilized world to consult the spirit of Apollo and to leave him magnificent offerings.

Omphalos of Delphi as it appears now.

Plutarch, who, during his latter years was a priest at Delphi, wrote in the second half of the first century A.D.: *It was not just a matter of some individual person consulting the oracle about the purchase of a slave or some other private matter, but of very powerful cities, kings and tyrants with mighty ambitions, seeking the god's counsel on important issues. To anger or annoy such men by harsh truths which conflicted with their desires*

*would have had its disadvantages. For this reason Apollo, though
not prepared to conceal the truth, manifested it in a roundabout
way: he clothed it in poetic form, thus ridding it of what was harsh
and offensive, as one does with a brilliant light by reflecting it and
thus splitting it into several rays.*

Then, Plutarch confirms, the messages became different. The
oracle seemed to be no longer limited to "complicated or secret
matters," but the Pythia answered questions "concerning people's
ordinary everyday problems." The writer, F.W.H. Meyers, adds:
*Greek oracles reflect for a thousand years the spiritual needs of
a great people. The Delphinian god became, in a certain sense,
the conscience of Greece.*

The oracle gave preference to Greeks and city-state magis-
trates who sought the oracle on all matters of public importance,
ranging from religion and law, prospects for the harvest, natural
disasters, the outcome of wars, and where and when to colonize.
Several officials were imported for the particular duty of visiting
the Pythia to ask questions, to ascertain how to conduct future
councils and fulfill the spiritual destiny of Greece. Weight was
certainly given to the replies received since they affected the lives
of all Greeks to a considerable degree. For Greeks, the oracle
acted as a sort of national barometer.

James Gardner (*The Fates of the World*) writes: *Its responses
revealed many a tyrant and foretold his fate. Through its means
many an unhappy being was saved from destruction and many a
perplexed mortal guided in the right way. It encouraged useful
institutions and promoted the progress of useful discoveries. Its
moral influence was on the side of virtue and its political influence in favor of advancement of civil liberty.*

With the powers he possessed, it is obvious that Apollo would
have become immersed in myth and legend. Somewhere along
the way he became labeled as a personification of the universal
deity, the sun, the regenerating principle which fertilizes Mother
Earth and causes the reproductive cycle. To link him to the mystical sun god only reinforces the idea that he came from outer

space, probably from Sirius or the Pleiades, which are themselves cosmic suns. Or perhaps even from the sun itself. We shall have much to say about the worship of the sun and the truth of its being the homeland of great beings. To call him a sun god, then, perhaps identified him with the solar deity of our solar system. He was labeled a world savior and he joined many other recognized god-beings as one who gave his life to the service of humanity, dying as a martyr for the cause of human progress.

The Oracle of Delphi
(from an ancient painting)

This drawing is from a book by J. C. Street, The Hidden Way Across the Threshold. *Mr. Street believed the cave of the Oracle contained a shrine housing an Ark of the Covenant. He further believed a voice spoke from the Ark giving guidance to the people. He believed the members of the group forming the crescent consisted of psychic persons. The five on the left of center were negative, those on the right were positive to balance the polarity. The Hierophant and three female psychics sat in the center. The Ark was a model of the Egyptian sacred boat and chest.*

Plutarch tells how the strange happenings of Delphi first came about. A shepherd named Kouretas noticed his goats leaping about strangely after being exposed to fumes from a deep chasm on Mt. Parnassus, around which lay the ruins of an ancient temple. Many persons flocked to the chasm to witness the actions of the goats. Some, coming too close to the fumes, fell into an ecstatic trance and began to prophecy. A few threw themselves into the fissure. Finally, the area was barricaded and a temple constructed especially for psychic and spiritual contacts. But the fumes still rose from the chasm, over which the Pythia sat to deliver the prophetic messages.

How striking the last graceful columned oracular temple must have been, surrounded by terraces, gardens and laurel trees. Lesser buildings belonging to the oracle dotted the slopes. Over the portico of this main shrine were painted and sculptured scenes depicting the triumph of humanity over evil forces. Hercules was there with his golden sickle—and Iolas, aiding Hercules to wither the heads of the dying Hydra. Zeus was there, crushing the Mimas with a great bolt of lightning fringed with flame. Also engraved there were two of man's great moral precepts—"Know Thyself," and "Nothing to Excess." The "Gnothi Seauthon"— know thyself—motto was attributed to Solon, the renowned lawgiver and one of the seven wise men of Greece.

At the entrance of the enormous cave-temple stood a gigantic statue of Apollo encased with gold leaf and crowned with the traditional laurel wreath. The circular main room housed many precious gifts, treasures of gold and works of art presented to the oracle by petitioners from all over the Mediterranean. The streets leading up to the temple were lined with monuments and rich treasures. There were over three thousand statues of bronze, marble and gold. Inside the temple was the hall of the Cinidians in which hung a most remarkable painting by the renowned artist Polygnotus. Cicero, the Roman philosopher and orator, beholding such splendor, wrote: *Never could the Oracle of Delphi have been so overwhelmed with so many important offerings from mon-*

archs and nations if all the ages had not proved the truth of its oracles.

Serpents carved in stone were very conspicuous in the sacred cave, which again alerts us to the realization that the cave had much to do with transformation of consciousness and raising the kundalini. Remembering the presence of the ureaus carvings in Egypt—heads of the upraised cobras which embellished the temples of the Mystery Schools of initiation—we are made equally aware that the subtle message of the transformation of kundalini energy was also evident at Delphi. The rows of the ureaus which adorned many of the sacred temples and Mystery Schools of Egypt—especially Zoser's Step Pyramid complex—signified that the temple was sacred to the secret Mysteries. The ureaus-cobra was also worn on the headdress of only the highest initiates. Serpents were equally in evidence in many of the carvings and statuary at Delphi, establishing it as a site of initiation into a Mystery School.

Delphi derives its name from Delphos, which means *the womb.* Indeed the cavern took on the shape of the female yoni. The vent leading into the depths of the Earth lent credence to this concept. The legend states that the sacred cave was supposedly the abode of the mysterious serpent, Python, who appeared after the great Flood had destroyed much of Earth's humanity. Apollo, ascending the side of Mount Parnassus, engaged in prolonged combat with the beast and eventually slew it and threw the body down the gaping fissure in the depths of the earth. Then the god took up his abode in the sacred cave to act as the divine oracle, offering guidance to mankind. The fumes arising from the fissure were reported to result from the decaying body of the great python.

But Apollo's struggle with the great serpent arouses a remembrance of the secrets of initiation in every temple of the Mysteries. One of the steps of initiation involved a struggle of the initiate with a serpent, sometimes actually living—but it symbolized the victory of the initiate over the serpent fire of kundalini, which lies slain and thrown into the crevice of the spinal cord where it lies dormant, coiled in the root chakra at the base of the spine. Raising the kundalini serpent fire to the crown chakra in the brain bestowed the highest form of illumination upon the initiate. It also established that the sex passion had been completely controlled and this tremendous force had been transmuted into the consuming spiritual flame by the awakened soul. The rising fumes supposedly from the decomposing body of the slain python at Delphi were reputedly responsible for propelling the priestess into a religious frenzy and trance.

Again we point to the awakened kundalini, whose "fumes" or essences rise up the spinal cord to cast the illumined initiate into a similar state. Striking the pineal gland in the third ventricle of the brain, the third eye opens to the mysteries of the cosmos, enabling the initiate to discern the future and the past—and to communicate with beings of the supernatural realms.

Thus the legend of Apollo's victory over a serpent established Delphi as a secret place of the highest initiation into the Greater Mysteries, long before it became an oracle.

But the story of Apollo slaying the dragon and depositing his body into the fissure or chasm in the mountain—and mysterious fumes rising from that chasm—holds another truth. When the gods of Olympus first arrived from outer space and established their abode on Olympus, they brought with them certain weapons as measures of defense against a barbaric horde of Earth's primitive humanity. They suspected the Eartheans might be hostile and violent. They knew, too, that the Titans had already arrived on Earth from another distant planet. So they came prepared for possible combat.

The weapon of Zeus, called his thunderbolt, was a lethal laser ray, far beyond laser weapons of today. So was the "bow and arrow" of Apollo. Among the weaponry brought to Earth was a "tank" type of weapon called a "dragon." It rolled over the Earth much as our present day tanks do—but it fired a laser ray. It gained its title as a dragon because it released a flow of destructive force similar to our flame-throwers. This tank-dragon was far superior to the clumsy tanks of our present weaponry. One of these weapons obviously fell into the hands of forces hostile to the gods. In the hands of unskilled Eartheans it was no match for Apollo with his renowned laser-arrows. In their struggle against Apollo the weapon fell into the wide chasm on the slopes of Mt. Parnassus.

After Apollo "slew the dragon," it was the uprising "fumes" from the fallen weapon which, inhaled by the goats, the shepherds, and later the Pythoness of the prophecies, that threw them into a state of ecstasy. The electromagnetic forces of the gridpoint kept the uprising force active. The vapor from the weapon's "eternal" laser ray was instrumental in causing a state of trance. The vapors arising from the chasm, reportedly from "the decaying body of the serpent, slain by Apollo," were actually a radioactive discharge from the fallen weapon. Again, Plutarch says: *The room in which those who came to consult the god were seated is, not often but occasionally and at irregular intervals, filled with a sweet-smelling vapor, as though the adytum were emitting as from a fountain the sweetest and most precious perfume.*

During the time of the oracles the Cave was most certainly inhabited by a great spiritual force which came to be recognized as Apollo, the sun god who came from outer space to serve the evolution of humanity. Having done so, he possessed the power to pour down atmospheric forces to unite with the earth's electromagnetic forces in the sacred Cave and the fissure of the earth—the Cave no doubt being the place of his initiation when he was victorious in raising the kundalini. The female priestess chosen to voice the prophecies and oracles—called the Pythia—became enraptured from the vapors rising from the fissure in the Cave, the fissure-chasm which entombed the fallen "dragon."

To prepare for prophesying, the Pythia first bathed in a natural spring—the Castalian—that sparkled down the mountainside. She abstained from all food. She drank only the water from the fountain of Cassotis, which was piped directly into the temple from a sacred well. This "water" contained the tinctures of herbal plants which helped to induce her trance—just as the soma drink was given to the neophyte seeking initiation into the Mysteries. Following the magical herbal drink, barley meal and laurel leaves were burnt before her. She chewed the bitter leaves of the laurel just prior to the ceremony to further induce her trance, and her attentive maidens crowned her with the wreath of these sacred leaves. She was clothed in sanctified robes. In a colorful procession the attendants escorted the Pythia to the shrine.

At the entrance the maidens departed and the prophetess entered the shrine alone. The circular main room, dark save for a few flames from the wall torches, was used for the ceremony. The priestess was seated in the center of the room on a tripod adorned

The Pythia sitting over the chasm to prophesy.

from the Manly P. Hall Collection, copyright Philosophical Research Society.

with laurel. The tripod, a kind of stool with three elongated legs—the twisted bodies of three enormous marble serpents—was placed over the mystic chasm from whence the uprising vapors issued. The three serpents forming the legs of the tripod symbolized the sacred Pythagorean tetrahedron. The Pythia seated at the apex symbolized the "capstone." As the vapors rose up to encompass the Pythia, the tripod vibrated as if reacting to some powerful physical force. Loud clanging echoed through the temple.

Inhaling the vapors the Pythia was seized with a strange madness. She struggled, she shivered, she tore at her clothes, she gripped the air, uttering strange cries. As she continued to inhale the mysterious vapors, slowly she became calm. Then a strange quietness possessed her as she passed into a catalytic trance—her body became rigid, her eyes staring fixedly into space. From her lips came the awaited prophecies. In the background sat the little band of five holy priests—"the Hosioi"—waiting to write down the enigmatic messages. Many were mutterings, but all were recorded by the attending priests. The words of Apollo, speaking through the divine madness of the Pythia, having been written down by the priests, were sealed and presented to the questioners, who came from all over the known world to seek guidance.

After completing the prophecies, the Pythia began her struggle again until she slowly regained her consciousness. She was carried bodily from the cavern and made to rest until all effects of her trance ecstasy had passed. Such trance states with their emotional upheavals, experienced several times a day, left the Pythoness totally exhausted. The life span of a Pythia was brief.

No one ever once accused the Pythoness of imbibing wine before prophesying. But she did freely imbibe the pure water of the Castalia Spring at the foot of Mt. Parnassus. The large drafts of water bathed in and drunk may have been holy water, made holy by the gods, as the waters of Lourdes have been made holy by the Blessed Virgin. They may have had their effect upon her. Also it is certain that she drank the Kykeon, the potent herbal drink which induced trance. The three reigning maidens who acted as the Pythoness were chosen because of their astonishing psychic abilities and their aptitude for entering a state of trance.

When one consulted the Delphic Oracle, one was required to observe a strict ritual. Those seeking answers were taken into the chresmographeion, a room where "applications" were received. Native Greeks were always admitted before foreigners. Lots were drawn to determine the order in which the petitioners were admitted. First, petitioners sought purification in the Castalia Spring which still flows not far from the ruins of the temple. The petitioner, after purification, was given a sacred cake to be placed on the main altar outside the temple. Then a goat was sacrificed to Apollo, after which one waited one's turn to enter the adytum, the hallowed precinct.

His first view would be of the enormous statue of Apollo flanked by two eagles, symbolic of the eagles dispatched by Zeus to locate the symbolic center of the Earth. The eagles were of solid gold and the statue of Apollo was also etched with pure gold. The adytum also contained Apollo's lyre and sacred armor. A laurel tree grew in a prominent place in the midst of the adytum. There, too, was found the tomb of Dionysus. In the adytum sat the Pythia on her tripod.

Often the question in written form was handed to one of the priests, who in turn put the question to the Pythia. Or it had been orally disclosed to the priest prior to the ceremony. The reply given by the Pythia was always written down by the priests.

The idea that the priests influenced the answers isn't true, simply because they would each have needed to be a prophet, since the prophecies usually came true. The oracle was renowned for accuracy and astuteness. They would have needed spies in all the countries and districts which lay far beyond the boundaries of Greece. They would have had to be aware of important passing events in even far-off villages, as well as the political picture in the palaces of kings.

In defense of the priests, the 19th century translator, Thomas Taylor, wrote in his *The Arguments of the Emperor Julian Against Christians: How is it possible, even if these priests had been a thousand times more cunning and deceitful than they were supposed to have been, that they could have such a secret so impenetrable in every city and province where there were any oracles as never to have given themselves the lie in any particular? Is it possible that there never was one man among the priests of so much worth as to abhor such impostors?—that no man should have ever explored the sanctuaries, subterranean passages and caverns where it is pretended they kept the machines?—that they should never have had occasion for workmen to repair them?— that only they should have the secret of composing drugs proper to create extraordinary dreams?*

And lastly, that they should have perpetually succeeded one another and conveyed their machines and the juggling tricks to all those that were to follow them in the same employment from age to age, generation to generation, and yet no man to have been ever able to detect the imposition? Besides, who were these priests that, as it is pretended, were monsters of cruelty, fraud and malice? They were the most honorable men amongst the heathens and, as such, were most esteemed for their piety and probity.

Plutarch—one of the most enlightened philosophers of Greece—presided as a priest over the oracle at Delphi. Depraved as humanity is, will anyone be hardy enough to ascent that a man of such probity, of such gravity, of such manners, of such penetration, learning and judgment, was a cheat and impostor by profession? The priests were carefully recruited, coming from noble families or from among the philosophers. They need have no qualifications as a prophet, but they were required to be highly intelligent and possessing psychological insight.

Occasionally a messenger from an important personage was dispatched to carry a petition to the oracle in a sealed tablet. Heavy punishment was dealt to such a deliverer if it was discovered that he had opened the petition before delivery. Responses to the petitions were always given in the strictest privacy, the contents never being revealed to any other person. When they were to be dispatched at a distance, again they were sealed. Liberation of the female certainly had not occurred at that time since only men could observe the ritual to ask questions. Women who sought the oracle had to employ a man as a go-between.

Those seeking guidance entered with an attitude of reverence, sometimes awe. Often visitors were crowned with a laurel wreath and given a branch of laurel to hold during the ceremony. A fixed minimum fee was charged. Occasionally one paid more to obtain priority if there was a need for urgent guidance. Once a year, for the benefit of the poor, a free mass oracle was held. The Pythia would sit on the temple steps in the open air and answer queries put to her.

Philostratus, in writing about the life of the renowned Apollonius, mystic, prophet and healer of Tyana, relates how he visited Delphi with his disciple Damis. His petition inquired if his name would be remembered by posterity. Philostratus states how, *when the power of the god came upon the Pythia her bosom heaved and she panted. Her face reddened, then was drained of color. Her limbs jerked and quivered and her eyes blazed. Saliva frothed on her lips, her hair stiffened and she snatched off her headband. She seemed possessed by some entity.*

Then she started to speak in a strange tone and the priests on either side wrote down her words and gave Apollonius the inspired communication. The Pythia replied that his name would indeed be remembered, but not for the good he had done. The prophecy angered Apollonius considerably, but it turned out to be correct because the early church fathers of Christianity, realizing that his stainless life and his astonishing miracles rivaled those of Jesus the Christ, labeled him as the antichrist. They attempted every type of blight on his name but they could never erase the record and the memory of all his miracles and the purity of his life. So the Pythia's prophecy was correct—his name was indeed remembered, but few were and are aware of the astonishing miracles of his life.*

King Aegeus of Athens came to Delphi, seeking to understand why he and his wife remained childless. The oracle said: *Loose not the jutting neck of the wineskin until you have come again to Athens*—which could have been interpreted to mean he should avoid sex until he returned home. Instead, you will recall, he was persuaded by the king of Troezene to mate with his daughter, Aethra, which resulted in the birth of a most famous son, the renowned Theseus. Perhaps the warning to avoid wine could have meant that imbibing wine would have made him temporarily impotent, thus preventing his mating with Aethra.

Phalanthas, king of Sparta, sought advice concerning his campaign against Italy. He was told that he should not attack until he felt rain fall from a clear sky. He ignored the advice and attacked Italy again and again. His invasions met with failure until one night, discouraged, he lay his head in his wife's lap. She, anguished at the thought of another of his campaigns, wept openly, her tears falling like rain upon his face. Sudden enlightenment dawned: her name, Aithra, meant *clear sky*, from which "rain" had fallen upon his face. He immediately attacked and captured the city of Tarentum.

Nero, emperor of Rome, consulted the oracle only to have the Pythia accuse him of murdering his mother. *Your presence defiles me!* she defied, *Begone, matricide! Beware of seventy-three!* Enraged at her refusal to honor him, he had the priestess buried alive, together with the priests of the temple. He interpreted her last words to mean he would live another forty-three years and die at age seventy-three. But he died a year later. The prophecy alluded to Galba who, at age seventy-three, succeeded him as emperor.

---

*See *The Secret Wisdom of the Great Initiates* by Earlyne Chaney, available from Astara, P. O. Box 5003, Upland, CA 91785-5003 or from your favorite bookstore.

Epaminondas was warned by the oracle that his death would come from the sea, yet he died in a wood at Mantineia, which was called the "sea wood." Croesus was warned that if he went to war with Persia he would destroy a great empire. Rejoicing at an expected conquest, Croesus immediately attacked Persia, but his armies were almost totally vanquished. The empire that was destroyed was his own. Cicero sought counsel with the oracle expecting to be told of his future fame. Instead he was advised to seek a better self-opinion rather than "the opinions of the multitudes." The oracle advised Chaeremon that Socrates was "the wisest man in the world."

To digress, the night before Socrates met his principal disciple, Plato, he dreamed of a white swan. When he met Plato the following day, he recognized the dream as symbolic, a white swan being the symbol of the highest initiate of Ancient Wisdom. Plato became a devotee at Delphi. He felt that the fumes of the chasm induced a state of trance because reason and common sense were in eclipse, overshadowed by a kind of intuitive madness through which prophecies might be inspired.

Apollo held sway for centuries at Delphi, overshadowing and prophesying through the Pythoness, except for the three winter months. His brother, the god Dionysus, then took his place. Apollo journeyed to the lands of the North during his absence— the land of the Hyperboreans.

In the beginning of the Delphinian Oracle, prophecies were only issued every year on the birthday of Apollo—on the seventh day of the month of Bysios, today's mid-February to mid-March. But as fame of the prophecies spread far beyond the Greek Isles and the populace of the world descended upon the miraculous center, the ceremonies were held every month. The effect of the Delphinian Oracle upon the culture of the Greek people cannot be measured—indeed, its effect upon the entire world.

In those days, it was never questioned that the Delphic priestess truly entered a state of trance and that the voice of the great god Apollo spoke through her, issuing the profound predictions and prophecies. It was no light undertaking since kings from far lands visited and established their ongoing policies and politics based upon the prophecies issued at Delphi.

Apollo, through the Pythia, advised not only those from afar, but also the Delphinians. When Apollo discerned that Xerxes plotted on plundering Delphi in 480 B.C. he advised the Delphinians to leave the treasures of the temple unguarded and to flee to the hills, for Apollo *could, with help, protect his own.* Following this advice, the Delphinians left the magnificent treasures in the temples and watched from behind protective barriers as the plunderer's army approached to desecrate the temple and escape with its treasures. Instead the army sought a rapid retreat as huge rocky crags suddenly split off towering Mount Parnassus and descended upon the invaders. When Brennus, king of the Celtic Gauls, attacked Delphi in 279 B.C. again rocks split off and crashed upon the attackers. Fire also descended from the heavens through flashes of lightning.

But Delphi received no such protection in the 4th century when the Roman Emperors Nero, Sulla and Philomelus all plundered Delphi. Nero carted away 500 bronze statues and closed down the oracle after it had rebuked him. It was reopened by Emperor Hadrian. Again it was closed when Constantine embraced Christianity as the official religion of Rome.

There were many other oracles in Greece at the time—Dodona, Branchidae, Zeus Ammon, Trophonius and Amphiaraus. But almost all the important colonization done by the Greeks was done on the advice of the oracle at Delphi. The Pythia was responsible for sending the Greeks to found colonies at Syracuse, in Sicily, in Byzantium and in Thessaly. The oracle exerted tremendous influence in still another field. Because of its essentially religious character, it became the arbitrator of morality. Many of the Greek standards of human conduct originated in lectures given at Delphi.

This same procedure was carried out at Dodona. It was second in importance only to Delphi. Dodona was a temple formed of trees enclosed as a circle, just as the Druids of England did in later centuries. At Dodona a gigantic tree stood in the center. It was believed that Zeus himself spoke through the tree. A famous black dove occasionally alighted on the tree and spoke the prophecies, presumably again, the voice of Zeus. The priests of Dodona were called the *Selloi.* The populace was astonished when these sacred priests all suddenly mysteriously vanished. Spaceships again come to mind. After their disappearance the prophecies were carried on by three selected priestesses who interrogated the sacred trees and interpreted the messages while in a state of ecstatic trance.

At the same time, the Druids of Britain were experiencing their own ceremonies of prophecies under the spreading branches of the sacred oaks or in circles or ovals formed of gigantic unhewn stones, as at Stonehenge. The oaks were planted in a circular formation, creating a sacred grove. When the priests gathered to receive answers to important queries they had first to proceed through solemn purifications. Once gathered in the grove of the trees or stones they queried God or great devas, who dwelt in the trees themselves, or in the principal stone. The voices of humans spoke, seemingly from the principal tree or stone, answering in prophetic fashion the questions of the priests. Usually, the voice came from one special oak tree or stone which stood in the very heart of the grove.

Nero abolished the Oracle of Delphi after Apollo, through the Pythia, had rebuked him for the murder of his mother. When it was reopened by the Emperor Hadrian it had lost much of its appeal since its desecration and plundering. The Christian Emperors had instilled fear in the hearts of would-be seekers of the prophecies, especially after Nero had a Pythia and the presiding priests buried alive. When Constantine the Great (273-337 A.D.) became emperor he ordered much of the magnificent statuary of

Delphi brought to Constantinople. The incomparable bronze serpents with the golden tripod and the seat where the Pythoness had sat over the mysterious chasm was removed by Constantine and placed as an ornament to decorate the Hippodrome in Constantinople.

When the Emperor Julian was born at Constantinople in 331 A.D., Constantine, his uncle, had already embraced Christianity as the official religion of the Roman state. Julian, however, having been initiated at Eleusis and again at Ephesus, only gave lip service to the new Christianity. He still believed in initiations, and the miracles and magicians of the Mystery Schools. When Constantine died and Julian became Emperor, he went about restoring the ancient shrines. He especially attempted to revive Delphi. But when he sent a messenger to Delphi to inquire of Apollo as to the future of the temple, he received from the oracle itself this message: *Tell the king that on earth has fallen the glorious dwelling and the water springs that spake are quenched and dead. Not a cell is left the god—no roof nor cover. In his hand the prophet laurel flowers no more. The Oak Hall has fallen to the ground. No longer has Thebus a hut. Nor a prophetic laurel. Nor a spring that speaks. Even the water of speech is quenched.* The prophecy was a true one. Never again did the oracle rise. Nor did Julian reign long. Before he had an opportunity to totally restore the Mystery Schools, he was murdered.

The oracle shrine was totally destroyed by the Christian Emperor Arcadius in 398 A.D. Until then Delphi shared the history of the world. The ruins lay untouched for more than twelve hundred years—until in 1671 serious archaeological excavations began.

Today Delphi once again is a shrine for pilgrims. They seek not prophecies as before. They seek only to experience a contact with the unseen—feeling through its impressive and awesome ruins and aura the actual overshadowing presence of the great god Apollo, and perhaps a maiden Pythoness who once served there. The sensitive mystic-initiate of today may still feel the uprising

currents of the Holy Node's umbilical cord, like the Ladder of
Jacob ascending into heaven—and the downflowing ethers of
spiritual essences as the angelic forces, treading up and down the
Ladder, strive to baptize the seeker in still-potent graces. And if
one listens well, s/he may catch the whisper of a long-vanished
god, chanting again the odes of welcome to one who, perhaps,
sought initiation long ago in the Cave of the Shining Crags.

Earlyne and Robert Chaney with their daughter, Sita, at Delphi.

The Tholos at Delphi— those sensitive to the ancient energies which dominated such sites as Delphi may still feel it surging through their bodies until they actually feel like human spirals.

The walls at Delphi are constructed with no mortar— each massive stone is dovetailed to create an eternal monument to Apollo, who prophesied here through the Pythoness for hundreds of years. Could the same Builders who built the incredible fortress of Sacsahuaman and Machu Picchu in Peru have built this holy site of initiation in Greece?

Apollo—the god whose dynamic presence is still felt at Delphi.

Chapter Seven

The Glory of Ephesus

That which is called the Christian religion
existed amongst the ancients and never did not
exist, from the beginning of the human race
until Christ came in the flesh, at which time the
true religion which already existed began to
be called Christianity.
—St. Augustine

In the distant past, long before the advent of Christianity, the city of Ephesus was chosen as the site for a monument to Artemis, twin sister of Apollo. The site was chosen because it was an important point of contact between Earth and downpouring spiritual ethers of higher planes. The historian Metrophanes reported the soil of the region was so fertile that a single cluster of grapes was of sufficient weight to break down a wagon. Ancient Ephesus nestled in a coastal harbor of Asia Minor is now part of Turkey. It is near the historical city of Selcuk (Seljuk), ten kilometers from the Aegean Sea and 680 kilometers from Istanbul. Ephesus is sometimes called Anatolia.

It is difficult to say when Ephesus was first founded—or who founded the site. The oldest records state that the enormous women warriors called the Amazons founded the first site as a temple of initiation into the experience called the Mysteries. The great temple was first dedicated to the mother goddess Kybele or Cybele, later renamed Artemis.

The first temple of Artemis was constructed completely of marble. The roof was supported by 127 columns. The original temple was 342 feet long by 163 feet wide, adorned with metal ornamentation. The mysterious Builders of that first temple— built under instruction of the gods themselves—are still unknown. They were simply called the Dionysian Artificers, actually the first Masons. It was built to honor Artemis, but the Mystery drama presented there involved the goddess Demeter (De-me-ter) and her daughter Persephone (Per-sef-o-nee).

In those ancient days its Mystery School was renowned as a center for the study of all secret and hidden arts of magic. There the initiates of the Mysteries integrated the magic of antiquity with the updated mystical ceremonies of the inner Mysteries. A century and a half before the birth of Christ the Greek mathematician Phylon wrote the following: *I have seen the walls and hanging gardens of ancient Babylon, the statue of Olympian Zeus, the Colossus of Rhodes, the Lighthouse of Alexandria, the mighty work of the high Pyramids and the Tomb of Mausolus. But when I saw the Temple at Ephesus rising to the clouds, all these wonders were put in the shade.*

Phylon was establishing the Mystery School of Ephesus as the Seventh Wonder of the world. He saw a shrine to Artemis, Diana to the Romans, erected to betoken a repository of cosmic knowledge. So rich and powerful did Ephesus become that other nations coveted its splendor. Its very glory hastened its final fall. It should be remembered that all the ancient goddesses were actually symbolic of the Earth Mother as personified by Demeter, Cybele, Isis and others known as Artemis, Persephone, Hecate and Diana. All are moon goddesses, aspects of the female sym-

Ephesus In Her Glory

bols of intuition. It seems only natural that this temple at Ephesus, dedicated to the moon goddess Artemis, who personified hidden knowledge, would later be dedicated to the Virgin Mary, who is herself a moon goddess.

Lucius, initiate of Eleusis, said: *I address my prayers to Isis, whom I speak of as Demeter, Persephone, Diana, Venus and all the moon goddesses. She appears in a vision as a beautiful female, whose long, black hair hangs in ringlets over her divine neck. When she speaks, she says, 'The parent of universal nature attends thy call. The mistress of the elements, supreme of deities, queen of departed spirits, and uniform type of all the gods and goddesses, propitiated by thy prayers, is with thee.' She governs with her nod the luminous heights of the firmament, the silent depths of the shades below—one sole divinity under many forms, worshiped by the different nations of the Earth under many titles, and with various religious rites.*

Lucius was declaring that all the moon goddesses were one and the same, each a representative of the one supreme feminine deity, manifesting as different personalities.

Of Ephesus, H.P. Blavatsky writes: *Ephesus was a focus of the universal 'secret' doctrines, the weird laboratory from whence, fashioned in elegant Grecian phraseology, sprang the quintessence of Buddhistic, Zoroastrian, and Chaldean philosophy. Artemis, the gigantic concrete symbol of theosophico-pantheistic abstractions, the Great Mother Multimamma, androgyny and patroness of the 'Ephesian Writings,' was conquered by Paul; but although the zealous converts of the Apostle pretended to burn all their books on 'curious arts,' enough of these remained for them to study when the first zeal had cooled off.*

It is from Ephesus that spread nearly all the Gnosis which antagonized so fiercely with the Irenean dogmas of Christianity. And still it was Ephesus, with her numerous collateral branches of the great college of the Essenes, which proved to be the hotbed of all the Kabbalistic speculation brought by the Tannain from the captivity.

Paul at Ephesus. During his stay he commanded his zealous disciples to burn all the sacred manuscripts of the Ephesus Mystery School, all the secrets of the rites of initiation. Yet, he later integrated many of these teachings into Christianity. Perhaps he did not want the Mystery manuscripts immediately available for comparison.

Initiates of the Mysteries of Eleusis saw "the sun blazing at midnight" for them alone. Persephone, the divine Virgin, spoke to them. Such initiates were ever after assured of salvation beyond death if they continued to live as initiates. In other words, they entered ecstatic states and witnessed visions of the White Light and holy beings. Socrates said: *We owe it to the goddess of Ephesus that we do not lead the wild life of earliest man. And to them (the Mysteries) are due the flattering hopes which initiation gives us for the moment of death and for all eternity.*

To attain such a glorious status as "a saved initiate," it was realized that much more than initiation was needed. Five years of discipline and preparation were required for purification prior to initiation—and vows of continued purification and a life of service to the light following initiation. Murderers and slaves were denied access to this special initiation.

During the initiation ceremonies, there was a scenic representation of Tartarus (hell and purgatory) and the judgment of the dead—and also of the fair fields of Elysium—just as in Egypt. Especially did the Mysteries teach of the soul's immortality— and that any form of sin was invariably followed by suffering, pain and remorse. The body was discerned to be a prison for the soul—but never was the soul condemned to eternal banishment from heaven.

In the Ephesus initiation, Dionysus was the Liberator. Socrates again says: "The great consummation of all philosophy is Death. He who pursues philosophy aright, is studying how to die." And that is what was taught to the initiates of Ephesus — how to die; how to recognize death as the ultimate initiation. And that is what we teach our initiates today in the Mystery School called Astara.*

Proclus says initiation at Ephesus commenced by invoking the two great causes of nature, the Heavens and the Earth, because they represented the Father and Mother of all generations.

*See *The Mystery of Death and Dying* published by Samuel Weiser and available from your bookstore or from Astara, 800 W. Arrow Hwy., P.O. Box 5003, Upland, CA 91785-5003.

The Omphalos—the electromagnetic stone ensconced at the entrance to the cave of initiation—was called "the Speaking Stone," because it was a sending and receiving station for communication between the god, goddess or hierophant of the earthly Mystery School and the gods and goddesses of etheric Mt. Olympus. Too, communication could be established between initiation sites and the orbiting space station established and controlled by the Olympian deities.

As the symbols and scenes progressed, the initiate was led into a labyrinth of stygian darkness. His/her soul was terrorized by every kind of fear—representing the phantom thoughtforms of the threshold—until the moment darkness faded into light and s/he beheld the brilliant scene of Elysium, where enchanting scenes of meadows, the dance of the angels, voices and chants of the Muses of music were beheld. Then the Virgin gave birth to a divine Son who saved the initiate from all darknesses and led the soul toward the light blazing in splendor around the statue of the goddess. How all this was accomplished was never revealed, but it can be said that the initiate, as the soul, experienced symbolic death, resurrection and salvation.

The subterranean cave of initiation in which the second birth occurred was known as the *sacred room* from which sprang the reborn soul. S/he slept a living trance for three days and rose again, a reborn initiate, after which his/her life was dedicated to the service of truth. S/he wore afterward the insignia of the redeemed, the saved and was given a new name inscribed upon a small white stone worn upon the person ever after. S/he was instructed in the secret chants and prayers of the goddess. This much can be described of the ancient ritual, but just how these rituals were performed will forever remain concealed.

The tyrants and their followers who later violated the sanctuaries found only stone images and caverns. They never beheld the light of the goddess. The secrets and the priesthood of the Mysteries vanished with the destruction of the temples. Out of the tragic fall of the Mysteries came the secret teachings of the

Gnostics and the Kabbalists. They were cautiously taught by the devout Essenes, a branch of the Dionysian Artificers. The Mysteries of the great Artemis became the secret doctrine which is again today being distributed among those who seek her secrets.

Thus, the first Christians built their new religion on secret doctrines which were previously revealed only to initiates after many years of study and purification. It was Eusebius, one of the early Church fathers, who admitted that the gospels were taken from early books of the Essenes—which implies that the writers, the apostles Matthew, Mark, Luke and John, the followers of Christ were, themselves, Essenes.

It is notable that the buildings once consecrated to the gods and goddesses of the Mystery Schools were renamed to honor the activities and saints of the emerging Christian faith. Many conflicts between the Mystery Schools and Christianity occurred in the great theaters of the Schools. As a result of one of these conflicts, St. John was put into prison on the hill named after him. He was later forced into exile on the isle of Patmos.

Each of the early temples of Artemis at Ephesus fell to ambush and destruction. But a new temple was created every time. During the thousands of years prior to Jesus, wars raged around the port of Ephesus. It remained unfailingly a temple to Artemis even though diverse religious groups invaded it and attempted either to destroy it or make it part of their own faith. Long past the birth of Christianity, Ephesus remained a tribute to Artemis, although the Romans had changed her name to Diana.

The fourth temple of white marble surrounded by Ionic columns, which required over 120 years to complete, was begun by Croesus of the Lydians. It was this temple that elicited the earlier noted quote by Phylon and caused Herodotus to declare it to be the most magnificent temple in the world—the Seventh Wonder.

A century later, in 366 B.C., the temple was destroyed once more by a madman called Herostratus. He had the strange notion that he could make his name immortal by destroying the temple. The indignant populace joined together to rebuild the fallen shrine. As the indignation spread throughout the world, donations arrived from individuals, kings and leaders, from the rich and the poor. Kings vied with each other for the honor of contributing the greatest treasure to the temple. Alexander the Great offered an enormous sum on condition that the new temple be dedicated to his name. The Ephesians, seeking to placate the warrior, answered with admirable tact, "But how can one god dedicate a temple to another?"

The fifth and last temple was finished in 323 B.C. Its incredible columns soared sixty feet above the plain. Wondrous statues and paintings graced the temple. The great lintel, however, was so enormous that the architect, Dinocrates, despaired of lifting it and properly situating it safely. Because of his despair he was on the verge of suicide when the great goddess Artemis appeared to him in his sleep, promising that the lintel would be properly established. On waking, the architect found the lintel safely in place.

Little remains today of this magnificent temple—the fifth and final one to be built on this sacred site. At its zenith the enormous theater could seat fifty-seven thousand. But today the temple site offers little to connect it to the glory of yesterday. The unearthed ruins, covering a site of twenty-six square miles, are mostly Roman. Only a quarter of it has now been excavated. There can still be found the Magnesia Gate and the marble street twelve yards wide leading to the site of the temple. Occasionally one glimpses the impressive headless statues. Only imagination can visualize the arcades where shops were once busily occupied. Temples and fountains can be discerned, six foot high tablets inscribed with the city laws, public baths, carved sidewalk inscriptions. It sits about three-quarters of a mile outside the walls of the city of Ephesus. Fig gardens and modern industry now surround the great shrine.

Reconstruction of the city, whose population must have exceeded several hundred thousand, progresses even today, though frequently hindered by the earthquakes which regularly shake the area. Though the great temple itself has disappeared, nothing can

John on the Isle of Patmos

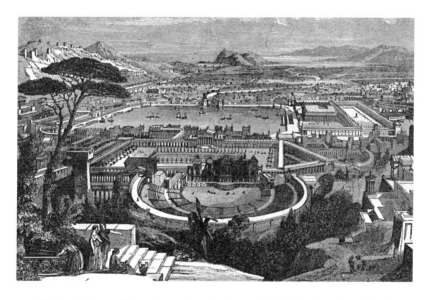

This artist's rendition shows how the theater looked in its prime. It had a capacity of fifty-seven thousand spectators and was the scene of one of the miracles perfomed by Apollonius of Tyana.

mar the grandeur of the landscape chosen by the ancient Builders as a perfect site for one of the most majestic shrines to the beloved Artemis/Diana.

Not only did the temple initiate those seeking initiation, but the School offered the teachings of a wonderful philosophy and mysticism, taught to disciples who gathered from the most distant parts of the world. So extraordinary was this Ephesian temple with its school of philosophy, it became the Mecca of initiates everywhere, sought by the Gnostics, the Neo-Platonists, and the sons of Manes of Egypt. In the cavern of initiation magical arts were taught and the sacred words revealed. These sacred words or chants were said to protect all who spoke them and were called upon in times of peril. Often they were written on lambskin or paper and worn as amulets upon the person.

Artemis, in whose honor the temple was built, was associated with the moon and the lunar cycle of generation. She was also the Virgin Mother of eternal wisdom, sustaining not only the human soul, but the World Soul. She was called the Mother of the Gods. Many of her attributes have long since been bestowed upon the Virgin Mary, the Christian Madonna. The fame of and devotion to Artemis rivaled that of Athena, the presiding deity of Athens. Standing in the temple was an immense wooden statue of the goddess. Like the Serapis of Alexandria, Artemis bore the various substances and materials derived from many species. One such statue was carved of ebony, so chosen because its darkness was supposed to be the home of eternal light. Some of the statues were formed of marble or alabaster—alabaster being associated with the lunar power.

The most familiar form of the statue depicts the goddess standing with feet together and body swaddled and bound. The hands are raised and spread in the attitude of healing. The many breasts which adorn her body speak of her powers as the goddess of fertility. A broad collar is ornamented with the signs of the zodiac. She wears a necklace of acorns, symbolizing the hidden seed of divinity in the heart of every soul. Her head is surrounded by a

The Goddess

nimbus, denoting the halo of glory. Artemis wears a turreted crown which speaks of her dominion over all terrestrial objects. Two lions adorn her upraised arms and her hair erupts in the form of flames. The various creatures adorning her form represent the creatures of nature. Often the statues had bronze hands, feet and head. She was often called Artemis Lucifera, the bringer of light and was also called the divine physician.

Except during initiatory ceremonies, the statues were normally veiled to protect them from the gaze of the uninitiated. During the initiatory ceremonies the veil was raised.

The Carpentum of Artemis was a sacred festival during which the image of the goddess was drawn through the streets, much as we now see processions carrying the Virgin Mary. On those momentous occasions the garments of the statue were magnificent vestments and robes embroidered with sacred and secret symbols.

The goddess is described by the words of Apuleius, an initiate of Ephesus: *Thou rulest the heavens round the steady poles. Thou illuminest the sun. Thou governest the world. Thou treadest on the dark realms of Tartarus. The stars move responsive to thy command. The gods rejoice in thy divinity. The hours and the seasons return by thy appointments and the elements reverence thy decree.*

When the Emperor Constantine declared Christianity to be the official religion of the Roman Empire, the worship of Artemis/Diana was forced underground, much to the sorrow of his nephew Julian, who later became emperor.

The Church today attempts to connect the miracles of the Mysteries with the use of drugs or as being produced by mechanical means or optical illusions. But even such accusations cannot erase the miracles of the goddess as she appeared during her festivals in one of her numerous aspects, giving oracles and bestowing enduring benefits. It was her incomparable appearance superimposing her own statue that appeared at the end of the initiation rites, filling the subterranean temple with a brilliance almost blinding the eyes of the initiates. During the process of initiation her statue often came alive, her divine presence stepping forth and walking among them, conferring the power of celestial vision upon special initiates. Initiates often reported seeing her in dreams and visions. These reports cannot be totally ignored else we must also ignore the miracles within our own faith.

Mary, the Blessed Virgin

Magnificent as it was, the temple at Ephesus never again attained its prior glory because those who rebuilt it never understood the original symbolism. It was first designed as a miniature of the universe, dedicated to the moon and to all the moon goddesses. It is little wonder that, following the crucifixion of Christ, the Holy Mother and St. John the Apostle sought refuge and retreat in this magnificent city on the Mediterranean. Surely they must have known that the Temple of Artemis/Diana at Ephesus marked that city as sacred to the Mystery religion.

Hearing Paul speak, Demetrius, a silversmith of Ephesus, gathered his colleagues together and declared that his craft was in danger and that the great temple of Artemis was about to be destroyed—the temple that all the world worshiped. So great was the tumult throughout the populace, Saint Paul was forced to leave for his own safety.

He later returned and spent five or six years there trying to convert the citizens toward Christianity in his ongoing workshops. John, too, came bringing Mary, the mother of Jesus, with him. John spent the latter years of his century-long life there, wrote the Book of Revelations there and on the isle of Patmos and was buried within the vicinity of the Mystery School at Ephesus on Ayasuluk Hill. In the first half of the 6th century A.D., Emperor Julian constructed one of the most magnificent monuments of the Middle Ages over John's tomb. Its ruins are there today, visited by many tourists.

The fourth book of the New Testament of the Bible, the gospel of John, was written in what is now the Church of St. John near his tomb in Ephesus. Even in the days immediately following the saint's death, the populace flocked to his tomb in hopes of a healing miracle. Healing water flowed near his tomb. The village once called Ayasuluk is now the city called Selcuk.

After the crucifixion of Jesus, life for his mother and his disciples became exceedingly dangerous. So John took Mary, as his mother, to Ephesus. There she dwelt in a small home nestled in a peaceful, quiet valley.

After her death the first Christian church was built at Ephesus. It was at the Third Council at Ephesus in the year 313 A.D. that the church was dedicated to Mary and called the Church of St. Mary. In the year 431 A.D. 111 general consuls and 318 bishops gathered for one of the most important events in Christian history. Here, in the Church of St. Mary, the momentous decision was made to refer to the Virgin Mary as the Mother of God rather than the Mother of Jesus.

Earlyne and Robert with their daughter, Sita, at the tomb of St. John.

The home of Mary at Ephesus, which has now become a chapel.

Chapter Eight

The Orphic
Mysteries

Orpheus was said to be the son of Apollo and Calliope, one of the Muses of Mt. Olympus. Though later writers declared that Orpheus came from Thrace, a cold and forbidding land, earlier writers spoke of his descendence from *Thracia*, which means "ethereal space." Thus, rather than hailing from Thrace, Orpheus descended from the legendary land of Thracia, which is not a geographical territory on Earth but which symbolizes the higher planes of life, or even some distant solar system. Thracia was called "the home of those who brought music and poetry to Greece."

Thracia was linked with "the Land of the Hyperboreans," the mysterious land thought to be partially on the etheric plane, presumably located near the North Pole, where eternal spring once reigned before a shift in the poles occurred. Hyperborea was also believed to be a favorite abode of Apollo, who departed Delphi every winter to seek the lands of the north, the tropical paradise on Earth. From this land his son Orpheus descended to bring wisdom to Earth. After the pole shift, Hyperborea became "the country that extended beyond Boreas, the frozen hearted land of snows and hurricanes."

The Hyperboreans are supposed to have entered the opening at the North Pole to establish a paradise inside the Earth. When they journeyed to inner Earth they found a muted sun shining in the center of the Earth, giving eternal spring to that undiscovered country. They journeyed there to avoid destruction of the pole shift. There, inside the Earth, they built their cities, the principal being Shamballa. There they have lived for eons. From there have come some of our UFOs. From there, too, have come great teachers, gods and goddesses, teaching Eartheans the Way to the light, guiding a primitive people toward enlightenment.

Of Orpheus, Thomas Taylor wrote: *As to Orpheus himself, scarcely a vestige of his life is to be found amongst the immense ruins of time. For who has ever been able to confirm anything of certainty of his origin, his age, his country and condition? This alone may be dependent on general assent. But there formerly lived a person named Orpheus, who was indeed the founder of theology among the priests, the instituter of their lives and morals, the first of prophets and the prince of poets. He himself was the offspring of a Muse. He taught the Greeks their sacred rites and Mysteries. From his wisdom has sprung the perennial and abundant fountain—the divine Muse of Homer, the sublime theology of Pythagoras and Plato.*

Somewhere along the way, as with the other gods, as the centuries passed, Orpheus ceased to be a human personality and took on the qualities and attributes of divinity. And truly, no vestige of history relates his actual origin, the time of his birth, his age, or any of the conditions of his birth. He simply appeared on Earth as singer of songs and creator of melodies—which were only two of his innumerable attributes and talents. So divine was he, he was without doubt a spaceman, arriving on Earth from some distant planet or from the etheric planes of Hyperborea to aid in the evolution of Earth's human lifewave.

He made his music on a seven-stringed lyre, given to him by Apollo, his father, which placed those who listened under a hypnotic spell. The lyre was first made by Hermes, who gave it to Apollo. The lyre "embraced the universe"—each string contributing to the Music of the Spheres. In the hands of this strange new god—whose golden hair fell in waves over his shoulders and whose deep blue eyes, shining with power and magic, "combined the arrows of the sun and the kisses of the moon"—the music of his lyre still reverberates among the stars.

The lyre has many mystical symbols and symbolic interpretations. It is known as the sevenfold mystery of initiation. The Pythagoreans regarded it as the symbol of the harmony of the seven planetary spheres, vibrating in resonance with the Music of the Spheres. It was also thought of as "evolving nature and the mysteries of divine creation," which simply tells us there are mystical sounds which will elevate the consciousness of the light seeker to harmonize with the vibrations of the oversoul.

Edouard Schure in his book *The Great Initiates* tells us how: *within the sanctuaries of Apollo, which held to the Orphic tradition, a mysterious festival was celebrated at the spring equinox. It was then that the narcissus burst yearly into flower near the fountain of Castalia on Mt. Parnassus near Delphi. The tripod on which the Pythia sat and the lyres of the temple gave forth quivering vibrations of their own accord and the invisible god, Apollo, was regarded as returning from the country of the Hyperboreans on a chariot drawn by swans.*

Then the high priestess in the garb of a Muse and wearing a laurel leaf, her forehead girt with sacred fillets, in the presence of none but initiates, chanted The Birth of Orpheus, son of Apollo and of a Muse. She invoked 'the soul of Orpheus, father of mystics, melodious savior of men, sovereign immortal Orpheus, thrice crowned—in hell, on Earth and in heaven—moving among the constellations and the gods, a star shining on his brow'.

As the first initiated adept recognized in the study of the Mysteries, Orpheus is known to have established many Mystery Schools and to have brought the secrets of initiation to the evolv-

ing souls and seekers in those prehistoric eras. He lived approx-
imately 7000 B.C. Legends make it very clear that Orpheus visited many nations teaching the wisdom and sciences of initiation.

When Virgil wrote of initiation into the Mysteries in his poem
"Aeneid," he describes the journey of the initiate Aeneas in his
trance state, his out-of-body experience. Aeneas *first penetrates
the dark realm of Hades, meets and conquers Typhon the serpent,
then ascends to the incomparable meadows of the Elysian fields.
There he beholds Orpheus clothed in a shining white garment,
touching gently the strings of his golden harp with an ivory thim-
ble.* It was not unusual for the initiate to witness heavenly planes
and come "face to face" with the gods and goddesses, or to behold
"the sun at midnight" during their three-day journey out of the
body.

There is no doubt that Proclus, Pythagoras, Plato and Homer
all accepted Orpheus as a living being with the soul of a god.
Pythagoras was greatly influenced by his teachings and wisdom.
So was Homer. The writings of Plato are sprinkled with his
teachings. H. P. Blavatsky maintains he existed as a living historical being and describes him as "the first initiated adept of
whom history catches a glimpse in the mists of the pre-Christian
era." Madame Blavatsky identifies him with Arjuna, the son of
Indra and disciple of Krishna in India.

An important part of the discipline in the Orphic Mysteries
was training in the interpretation of the Mysteries in symbol and
allegory, which contained the secrets of the workings of nature,
the powers of the universe and the faculties of the soul. He established as the highest purpose of the Mysteries the attainment of
real spiritual awareness. He was also the founder of theology and
laid down many guidelines for the morals of the ancient Greeks.
He was recognized as a great prophet, a prince of poets and wise
in the Grecian sacred rites and Mysteries.

When he was still young, Orpheus—along with Herodotus,
Thales, Pythagoras, Plato, Parmenides, Empedocles and many
others—traveled to Egypt seeking the secrets of Egypt's Mystery

Schools. After twenty years he returned with a profound knowledge of magic, astrology and medicine, bearing the initiate name of Orpheus or Orpha, which means *he who heals with light*. He not only developed the power of healing, he perfected his skill in music. He was also an initiate of the Mysteries of the Cabiri (Kabe-ri) at Samothrace, which added to his knowledge of medicine and music. Orpheus emphasized the divine nature of man, personal responsibility, his purity and even his divinity. Living the highest of one's potential divinity was called "living the Orphic life."

Raphael

The Mystery School at Athens

The Orphic religion emphasized belief in reincarnation. He taught that the souls who were destined for rebirth were required to drink from the Waters of Lethe—or the waters of forgetfulness—so that a veil concealed the memory of previous lives and all that they had experienced since their last death. Only when the soul had overcome the cycle of reincarnation had that soul attained the ability to know and remember everything.

Orpheus rivaled Hermes as a prolific writer. Among his writings was one dealing particularly with various mystic rites. One was called *The Enthronings of the Great Mother,* which seems to refer to a rite known as *Incathedration.* During this ceremony the adepts enthroned the candidate and circled round him/her in a ceremonial dance symbolic of the influence of the oversoul toward the spiritual progression of the neophyte.

His secret writings called *The Sacred Vestiture* and *The Rite of the Girdle* describe initiations of the candidates as they were invested with a band or cord of gold which reminds us of the sacred Brahmanical thread and the Kusti thread of the Parsee, still practiced in India today. The best known of his writings are the *Hymns of Orpheus* which number eighty-six, all directly connected with the divine Mysteries. Many who followed after him, especially the Kabbalists, extracted secrets of magic from the hymns. Apollonius declared that the "followers of Orpheus should be called magicians."

He was a teacher of *Mantra-vidya*, in which he disclosed the charm and magic of the mantra. He composed an alphabet and a system of hieroglyphics and symbols. He wrote many direct prophecies and oracles. One of his writings devised the means of purifying soul and body. He was a supreme initiator. Proclus declares that "all the theology of the Greeks comes from Orphic Mystagogy." Pythagoras based much of his teaching upon the philosophy and religion of Orpheus. And Plato referred frequently to his writings, which stressed the one supreme God.

Plato

He acknowledged that wild beasts were charmed by his divine melodies. And it was also true that men and women who possessed a wild and unruly nature were brought back to a life of love and light, through not only his music but his writings. He not only taught of the mystic ritual but how to master the art of healing.

He spoke of the divine Essence which is inseparable from whatever *is* in the infinite universe, all forms being concealed from all eternity in it. He taught that through the law of evolution, all forms and all things participated in this divine Essence, which was and is omnipresent. He taught that since all things trace their source to the divine Essence, all things must necessarily return into it, but that the return journey involved innumerable incarnations and purifications. He taught of a final consummation. This sounds remarkably like pure Vedanta philosophy.

He joined the greatest heroes of Greece to sail on the Argo with Jason to seize the Golden Fleece. With his music he soothed stormy seas, and saved the Argonauts from the lure of the Sirens. The Sirens were scheming enchantresses who lured sailors to their destruction through their unearthly melodies. Orpheus outdid them by playing such divine melodies that none of the Argonauts fell victim to the Sirens. He lulled to sleep the dragon of Colchis so that Jason might seize the Golden Fleece.

Myths and legends are interwoven throughout the history of his life—for instance, the romance and marriage of Orpheus and Eurydice (You-*rid*-di-si), whom Orpheus loved dearly. Eurydice was a Dryad—a nymph of oak trees. The life of each Dryad was associated with that of her own tree in which her soul force lived. While fleeing from an assiduous assault of Aristaeus, the villain seeking to seduce her, Eurydice was stung on the heel by a poisonous serpent from which she died.

Devastated, Orpheus penetrated to the depths of the underworld seeking her release and resurrection. By his music he subdued Cerberus, the three-headed monster-guardian of the gateway to the netherworld. He came before Hades and Persephone, playing his wondrous music. So enchanted were they, they agreed to permit Eurydice to return to life if Orpheus would go before her and not look back until they both had reached the sphere of the living—to which Orpheus agreed. But so great was his anxiety that Eurydice might become lost along the way, he turned to look upon her and she was immediately returned to the land of the dead.

"Quick from his eyes she fled in every way, like smoke in gentle zephyr disappearing" (Virgil).

The myth isn't clear as to what happened to Orpheus after the loss of his beloved Eurydice. He turned his back on all women. Some of the myths declare that he committed suicide. Some say he was slain by Zeus with a bolt of lightning for revealing to mortals too many of the secrets of the sacred Mysteries. Some say he was assaulted and torn to pieces by a group of women of the Bacchic procession, whom he had rejected. In a frenzy of their mystical orgy, they assailed him, tore his body to pieces and scattered them over the Earth. This is the same fate which befell the divine Dionysus—and also Osiris, the highest divinity in the Egyptian Mysteries, who was murdered and mutilated by Set, the power of darkness. The body of Osiris too was scattered over the land along the Nile.

These mutilations of the highest forms of deity point to the mystery of creation and the fragmentation of the one supreme deity, or the One Life, into multiplicity or diversity. The resurrection of these gods, with the assembling of the scattered parts and the restitution of the body, symbolizes the reintegration of the separated souls of humanity into the unity of the One Life. The Church ritual of the sacrament of the holy Eucharist embodies this mystery of the Mystery Schools, though the Church has long since lost its true meaning. The breaking and partaking of bread—or wafer—representing the divine body of Christ, and the distribution of the fragments among the devotees as "consuming the body of Christ," is a reenactment of a secret ritual from the

Mysteries, where the neophytes absorbed the body of Dionysus, Orpheus or Osiris.

Mythologists declare that when the Bacchanals assailed him the head of Orpheus separated from his body and was cast, along with his lyre, into the river Hebrus. The river carried it toward the sea. Near the sea it lodged in an oracular shrine on the island of Lesbos and gave oracles for many years—that is to say, prophecies. The lyre was rescued by the gods and taken among the stars to be formed into a heavenly constellation.

Now what is the interpretation of this mystical tale? Blavatsky offers: *The fable of the shepherd, Aristaeus, pursuing Eurydice into the woods where a serpent occasions her death is a very plain allegory. Aristaeus represents brutal power pursuing Eurydice, the esoteric doctrine, into the woods of darkness where the bite of a serpent, emblem of every sun god, kills her—that is, the brutal power of the profane, who do not understand the true purpose of initiation, forces the truth of initiation to become still more esoteric and seek shelter in the underworld. The fate of Orpheus, torn to pieces by the Bacchanals, is another allegory to show that the gross and popular rites are always more welcome than divine but simple truth, and proves the great difference that must have existed between the esoteric and the popular worship— between the Greater Mysteries and the Lesser.*

In the kingdom of Hades, Orpheus seeks Eurydice, his lost soul. The descent to the underworld is a myth common to the legendary lives of many gods and heroes and was enacted during the Mysteries of initiation. The hidden meaning of the rite was the incarnation of the soul in the shadowy realms of matter. The returning to light alludes to the liberation from the bonds of flesh. Those who had gone through the trials emerged from the dark regions of "the dead" as adepts and saviors of humanity.

Having nearly reached the upper world, Orpheus looks back and Eurydice dissolves into a mirage and floats away. This means that man cannot contemplate truth before gaining light or illumi-

nation. If he tries to seize it within the darkness of his ignorance, truth vanishes.

Blavatsky, again maintaining that Orpheus is identified with Arjuna, states that the very story of his losing Eurydice and finding her in the underworld of Hades, is remarkably similar to the story of Arjuna who goes to Patala (Hades or hell, but in reality the Antipodes, or America) and there finds and marries Ulupi, the daughter of the Naga king.

The dismembered body of Orpheus symbolizes the various factions of reality which tear apart the body of truth. That his head continued to live and prophesy symbolizes that truth itself can never be destroyed regardless of the fragmentations created by theology. The lyre of Orpheus containing the seven strings represent the seven initiations leading toward individualized godhood. Since the disappearance of Orpheus remains a mystery, could it be that following the death of Eurydice he entered a spaceship and returned to the mysterious land from whence he came?—perhaps to some distant planet or to the etheric realms of the Hyperborean.

Since Apollo, father of Orpheus, is a mythological representation of the secret doctrine, this mystical teaching reveals that Orpheus, an offspring or branch of Apollo, was a branch of the secret wisdom taught through music. Eurydice represents humanity, imprisoned in the world of matter through the sting of the serpent, or the downward flowing energies of the kundalini to the generative organs which stimulate physical sexual desire and which holds the soul to physical rebirths—as opposed to the uprising kundalini through the spine to seek the Holy Spirit. Again we have the serpent playing a vital double role in the Mysteries.

Orpheus, also representing humanity, failed to accomplish the resurrection of Eurydice because of an innate loss of faith in the promises of the gods. Plato's *Republic* states that at the time his soul sought rebirth in the physical world Orpheus chose to return in "the body of a white swan." This teaching emphasizes his personification of truth, since the white swan is the symbol of the highest phase of initiation and of the initiates of the Mysteries. In the Mysteries of India, only the highest initiate can assume the title of "white swan," or Hansa—which means Orpheus returned as an illumined savior, and came not because he had karmic debts to pay but because he chose to return to guide humanity. Perhaps Plato himself was Orpheus returned to Earth, since Plato was often called "the Swan" by his teacher Socrates.

In the story of the descent of Orpheus into the underworld to consult Hades concerning the liberation of Eurydice, we can discern the story of evolution and the descent of spirit into matter. We can also perceive the descent of the ego into the physical world as a personality.

We can also say Orpheus and Eurydice symbolized the united feminine-masculine aspects of the seeker of light, the harmony of love-wisdom. Orpheus goes to the rescue of his wife in the underworld. He confronts the lord of the underworld, Hades, to bargain for her resurrection, or return to life, by playing his divine music. Eurydice, symbolic of the soul in imprisonment in the lower realms of darkness, or matter, is held prisoner. It is the work of love or the oversoul to present the sounds or Music of the Spheres to gain her release, thus attaining the resurrection of the dead, or the liberation of the soul from rebirth in the physical realms. But, although the love aspect of Orpheus is enough to partially transmit the resurrection of Eurydice, he lacks the total quality of divine will. Faith and purpose are not yet mature. Thus, Orpheus looks back. The melody is aborted and the soul is again precipitated into matter—destined for rebirth on the physical level.

Could it not be that Orpheus, in his teachings of the Mysteries, presented himself as representing the oversoul who follows the soul—Eurydice—into matter, there to gain the soul's release from the wheel of rebirth in matter. But the oversoul itself, in its anxiety to bring about liberation for the soul, "looks back"—which means that instead of keeping its consciousness attuned always toward the cosmos, it allows its attachment to the soul and the soul's earthly conflicts to deter it, and the soul, instead of gaining liberation or salvation, returns to another incarnation in matter.

Such a myth would tell us that in most persons the oversoul—that house not made with hands, eternal in the heavens—has not yet reached its ultimate fulfillment. It can only do so by project-ing a part of itself, the soul, again into incarnation—for only through such experiences can the soul build further light sub-stance into completion of the body of the oversoul, the causal body. This could be the great wisdom Orpheus taught his initiates when admitting them into his Mysteries. Such an initiation would encourage the personality, the soul, to struggle harder toward light and love in order to build the oversoul toward perfection—for only through such perfection can the soul itself gain liberation (salvation) and attain its final release from the wheel of rebirth, forever after "to dwell with the immortals," those who need no longer become mortals.

But the serenade of his divine voice is penetrating all the kingdoms—the animal, vegetable, mineral and, indeed, that of mankind, as harmony, sound and prophecy. Civilization after civilization spreads over the face of the Earth, only to collapse whenever the basic accompaniment of wisdom becomes drowned in the chamber of faithless seeking. Mankind reverts very quick-ly to a natural depravity when sheltered too much from the down-pouring essences of Holy Spirit. Man's ultimate ascension must wait upon his capacity to receive and give forth the music of love-wisdom. The seeker must undertake not to look back. When enough seekers attune to the resounding Music of the Spheres, answering the call of Holy Spirit, only then will our civilization rise at last to the full music of the cosmic Maestro, infusing eter-nal life and evoking that which is immanent—the Holy Spirit.

The Golden Tablets of Orpheus

Genuine relics of the Orphic tradition are the famous golden tablets which have recently been discovered in various tombs, some of which were in southern Italy. The inscriptions engraved on them contain directions for the conduct of the deceased on his entry into the astral world, much as the *Book of the Dead* did for the Egyptian initiate. These tablets date from the fourth to the third century B.C. On one of those tablets it is written, "I'm a child of Earth and of the starry sky, yet my origin is in Heaven." And then the soul asks to be allowed to drink from the Waters of Mnemosyne or memory, to remember how celestial he was before he fell into the world of matter and rebirth.

In the golden Orphic tablets it is established again and again that there is a sharp dualism of body and soul. Thus the Orphic Mysteries, based upon the Dionysian myth, were involved in the process of salvation through purification from bodily taint, attempting to destroy the innate Titan influence. The Orphic initiates not only sought deliverance from the evils of present life but liberation from a long series of future bodily existences. This was the meaning and purpose of all the Mysteries and their initiates.

How was this great liberation to be accomplished? First, by participating in the rites of initiation, which could only be experienced through the process of purification. In the Orphic rites, eating a tiny portion of roasted flesh of the sacred bull and drinking the soma Kykeon had two important connotations. First, it was a holy communion service—a Eucharist. The initiate had within himself not only the spark of divinity, but also the low self of the Titanic influence. The divine life, being weak, needed nourishment. Eating the flesh of the sacrificed bull—symbolic of the roasted flesh of Dionysus—helped him to partake of the divine substance. He ate the substance of the sacrificial bull as Christians now eat the wafer-host to integrate within themselves the body of Jesus. And they drank the soma drink to symbolize partaking of the blood of Dionysus, as Christians drink the wine symbolic of the blood of Jesus.

It was Clemens of Alexandria who helped outlaw the Orphic Mysteries and its initiations based on the "heathen act of eating flesh and the drinking of wine"—establishing at the same time the Christian Eucharistic ceremony of eating the body of Jesus and drinking his blood. He called the Bacchic ceremony orgiastic and barbarian, while he made the Christian Eucharist the highest form of ritualistic Christianity. He based the Eucharist upon the statements of Jesus at the last supper, but he ignored that Jesus, greatest of all initiates, was simply carrying forward Dionysian initiation secrets.

Even after living a life of righteous conduct, the golden Orphic Tablets make clear that there are certain post-mortem activities to be observed. They recognize the spheres of the next world and they teach initiates of reincarnation, acquainting them with the divine Beings who will determine whether or not they will seek rebirth.

The Tablets further describe certain rituals to be observed, including repeated confessions. The way of salvation provided by the Orphic initiation, including an extended process of self-discipline, ended in a spiritual regeneration that broke forever the chain of successive physical births.

There were prayers to be constantly repeated, sacrifices to be fulfilled and sacraments of communion and purification following the initiatory rites. There was a rigid discipline of lifelong asceticism that included fastings, freedom from bodily contaminations, moral discipline, followed, again, by a post-mortem ritual, all of which certainly speaks of a purified "Christianity."

On one of the tablets found at Pelelia, the following verse was found:

> You will find to the left of the House of Hades a
>   spring,
> And by its side a white cypress standing.

Do not approach near this spring.
You will find another, with cold water flowing
From the Lake of Memory, and sentinels before it.
Say "I am a child of Earth and starry Heaven,
But my race is of Heaven. You know this already.
But I am parched and perishing of thirst.
Quick, give me the cold water flowing from the Lake of
          Memory."
Then they will freely let you drink from the holy
          spring,
And, after, you will have lordship with the other
          heroes.

This following verse is from Thurii:

I come in purity from a pure people,
          O Queen of the Dead,
Eucles, Eubuleus, you other immortal gods.
I too claim to be of your blessed race.
Fate and the star-hurled thunderbolt
          overwhelmed me.
I have flown out of the sorrow-heavy weary wheel,
I have moved within the crown I desire
          with eager steps.
I have sunk into the lap of Our Lady,
The Queen of the Dead.
Happy and blessed, you shall be a god,
          mortal no more.

In these verses alone we find teachings of the underworld, a system of passwords, directions for the soul following death, a teaching of reincarnation, attainment of liberation from the wheel of rebirth—or salvation for the soul—which meant the initiate had gained immortality and never again need to be reborn on Earth as a mortal. This initiate even implies aid from Our Lady, which is the title we now confer upon the Blessed Virgin of Christianity. He calls her Queen of the Dead. In our own mystical teachings we have pointed to promises made by the Virgin to those who persistently pray to her—assuring the devotee that she will be present at the hour of death to escort the soul across the threshold into the regions of light. Thus she surely could be titled Queen of the Dead. There must have been a celestial goddess similar to the Virgin Mary who aided the initiates during the time of Orpheus.

Orphism and Initiation Today

The rites of Orphism influenced the rites of the Eleusinian Mysteries. Perhaps that is why these Mysteries came to mean so much that they were continued for at least four hundred years after the birth of Jesus. Perhaps they even became the basis of the new religion called Christianity.

The purification and self-discipline begun through the Orphic initiation was a discipline and purification that lasted throughout a lifetime. Called "living the Orphic life," it reflected the initiations given in Egypt, closely followed by the school at Crotona under the direction of the Greco-Egyptian initiate Pythagoras. Both in life and in death, certain restrictions were observed in that the Orphic wore garments of pure white. Having once partaken of the tiny particle of roasted flesh of Dionysus during the rites of the Eucharist in initiation, symbolic of the body of a god, the Orphic afterward took the vow of vegetarianism, fasting forever from animal food. This abstinence from animal food was one of their principal disciplines.

Thus through fasting, purifications and the wearing of purified garments, the Orphic lived an exemplary life. The Orphic deplored the slaughter of animals for food. The sacred bull slaughtered for their Eucharist had been purified in every possible way. The Orphic initiates were renowned for their purity of living and practice of the highest virtues. The Orphic wisdom and way of life were taught by Pythagoras, and Plato's writings reflect the same doctrines.

During the day of initiation, the Orphic initiate was crowned with leaves of fennel and poplar. Often they carried a symbolic serpent in their hands, perhaps symbolic of the manner of Eurydice's death, perhaps symbolic of their awakened kundalini. During the ceremony they performed a ritualistic dance, at the end of which they were baptized in holy water. Their bodies were anointed with a special oil and clay. Then the skin of a young fawn was fastened over their clothing, symbolizing rebirth—the birth of the high self emerging from the animalistic self. Each initiate was given the promise of immortality and union with divinity at the time of death.

The Orphic initiate was taught that the body itself was a tomb from which the soul must seek liberation. Such release was obtained through the sacrifice of the lower passions and living a moral life. The initiate was taught that death released the soul from the tomb of the body, but the soul who had not attained full liberation would once again be imprisoned in a physical form. Thus Orpheus taught reincarnation and the grace of redemption. Dionysus was the savior sought in this teaching, as Jesus is our savior. Initiates were taught that by living a pious life their next incarnation would manifest upon a higher spiral until, through the ascent of destiny, the soul was eventually liberated from the physical plane.

From Bryant's *An Analysis of Ancient Mythology*

The Orphic Egg

The symbol of the Orphic Mysteries was the Orphic Egg, depicted as being entwined by a serpent with the head upward. This was interpreted to mean the cosmic egg encircled by a living fire—the creative spirit. The initiates were taught that at the end of each age the lifewave of mankind emerges from its embryonic stage to evolve toward mature understanding through initiation.

Could we but trace the influence of Orpheus upon every religion existent in the world today, we might pause, incredulous, to realize how his influence has persisted through the ages, from before the time of recorded history. We cannot help but realize that whoever Orpheus really was, he brought to Earth a wealth of wisdom applicable to us today regardless of our faith and our religion. He brought us emanations from a divine source, an outpouring of knowledge and wisdom which, though veiled from the profane, contained the Truth, the Way, and the Life for those who had eyes to see.

Only by studying the life and teachings of this astonishing "god-man" can we initiates of today's Mystery Schools realize the import he had and still has upon our faith, our wisdom, our philosophy, our own initiation and, indeed, our own soul liberation-salvation. The guidelines he taught then are still applicable today for initiates who truly seek their immortality.

Chapter Nine

The Eleusinian Mysteries

Today few sightseers visit the shrine of Eleusis, a small town near Athens. It is fallen indeed from its previous days of glory. Viewing it today, surrounded by a billowing pall of smoke, smog and busy day activities, it is hard to realize that at one time this undistinguished hamlet was a symbol of Greece's highest civilization. It was the site of the world's most renowned secret society—the wisdom of which was sought by everyone, wise and profane alike. In the great temple at Eleusis, the Mystery School presented the secret rites of initiation called the *Eleusinian Mysteries.*

The Mysteries are believed to have first been celebrated about fourteen hundred years before the birth of Christ. But we know, as with all the Mysteries, they had their beginning in the long ago mists of time, so long ago time has forgotten, when the space people first came—especially those embracing the worship of Demeter, goddess of agriculture and fertility. Demeter symbolized the Earth Mother Goddess. It was she who first instigated the Mysteries at Eleusis.

No historian or archaeologist has ever been able to establish when the Mystery Schools and their rites of initiation began in Greece. It's fairly clear that they first came through Crete and the Minoans. It's also clear that the space gods established headquarters on Crete before they ever came to Mount Olympus. It is most certain the Knossos palaces now excavated on Crete, with their strange chapels, halls and labyrinth, were indeed sites of initiation and the Mysteries.

Whether Eleusis was established through the Cretan rites no one knows. Obviously the gods moved from Crete into Mt. Olympus following the Thera earthquake, to establish their permanent abode. The only thing for certain is that the Greeks knew, believed in, and were familiar with the Eleusinian Mysteries since time began for them. Their origin has been traced back as far as the eighteenth century B.C. But even that tracing does not establish their beginning. It is known that the early structures included a megaroon, which is a sacred chapel or hall, much as the Masons now have a Lodge.

The grandeur of Eleusis developed through the centuries, resulting in the famed Telesterion, or ceremonial cave. Certainly these Mysteries were in existence during the fourteenth century B.C. and influenced the Minoan, Mycenaean and Thracean cultures.

From the earliest times the Mysteries were divided into two levels of understanding, the Lesser Mysteries for the populace, the Greater for the initiates. The Greater Mysteries, which initiated disciples into Ancient Wisdom and illumination, required purification, sacrifice, isolation and darkness, procession through a labyrinth and finally epiphany in the grand hall of Demeter.

Although little is known about the actual secret rites, it is known that the dramas and rituals included the teachings of death, rebirth and immortality, signifying being "saved" from rebirth. The Lesser taught the death of the seasons and the rebirth of the plant kingdom. The Greater taught of liberation of the soul and escape from the wheel of rebirth. The initiates experienced a three-day death ritual (trance) to be reborn or reawakened as a demi-god, a foreshadowing of their immortality after death. This sounds amazingly Christian. In fact, in the drama of the Mysteries there always was a Virgin Mother who gave birth to the savior for mankind. The Mysteries' greatest appeal lay in their promise of immortality after death for their initiates—if they led a light-filled life.

The initiation process required an entire year, the final rites being a nine-day celebration at Eleusis. Purification, sacrifice, entering a state of death-trance, exposure to visions, spiritual perception and ultimate crowning in the light were all a part of initiation. The candidates, groping their way through gloomy caverns of the soul's sublunar migration—the valley of the shadow of death—were reminded that the soul must pass through the underworld and be exposed to and redeemed from past sins before it can reach the heights of heaven.

In the Mysteries of Eleusis, death and rebirth, dying and coming into birth formed the central theme. At the conclusion of the rites, the symbolic birth of a divine child, Dionysus, was greeted with joy, the son of the Virgin Persephone, who, identical with her mother, Demeter, was goddess of agriculture. She was the spouse of Hades, which made her queen of the underworld. In the sacramental act of the Mysteries, the initiate met the goddess of the underworld herself—in that act descending into death and rising again to life.

Though called the son of a divine Virgin, Dionysus was also called the son of Zeus. Zeus in this case acted as the Holy Spirit, impregnating Persephone as the Holy Spirit impregnated the Virgin Mary. Like Jesus, Dionysus came forth as the savior of mankind.

The rites and celebrations of the Eleusinian Mysteries could actually be a reflection of the rites of Isis and Osiris of Egypt. It led the initiate toward attaining ultimate union with the divine, which was the goal of all initiations. The Mystery Schools were established to help each initiate attain that goal. It was certainly the goal in the Orphic, the Eleusinian, and in the Ephesus Mysteries. But then all the Mystery Schools had this one divine purpose. Their outer purpose was to interpret nature's most precious secrets. Their inner was to recognize these secrets within the soul and to bring that soul to its highest natural potential. The secrets of the Eleusinian rites were called ineffable, just as the Masonic rites are now, because they concerned the Universe. It means that they were unknowable by the ordinary mind. The Greater Mysteries held strictly to one purpose—the spiritual transformation of the individual initiate.

Frequently the sun god was involved with cycles of lunar and solar movements. In the Lesser Mysteries, the dying sun in winter symbolized the death of the season, and the sun's return meant the rebirth of vegetation. The Greater referred to the death of the sun to be reborn as a son of the sun god—the Sun, the Moon and Mercury were involved.

The drama of the Eleusinian Mysteries involved the goddess Demeter and her daughter Persephone—or Kore. Demeter was the daughter of Rhea and Cronus which makes her the sister of Zeus. Her daughter, born of Zeus, was Kore in the Lesser Mysteries. In the Greater, she was called Persephone. But only the Epoptes—the highest initiates—were allowed to speak of her as Persephone, which seemed to be a sacred name involving certain sounds whose pronunciation was not permitted by the profane.

The legend begins with Demeter, whose symbolic marriage to the god Zeus produced a most beautiful daughter, Persephone. Her angelic beauty attracted the attention of Hades, Lord of the underworld. The drama depicts Persephone picking flowers in a beautiful meadow. Attracted by a glorious narcissus, she strayed too far from her companions. In the midst of such beauty, the earth suddenly opens to admit the emergence of the god Hades riding in an elaborate chariot drawn by coal-black steeds. Seizing Persephone, and ignoring her cries which echoed through the high hills, he carried her to his palace in the subterranean depths. Demeter, hearing her cries, sped like lightning to the meadows to rescue her beloved child. But Persephone had totally vanished and no one would tell Demeter where she had been taken.

In the drama, grieving Demeter seeks everywhere for her lost daughter. In the Greater Mysteries, Demeter carries two torches, representing intuition and reason. The torches are to aid her search for Persephone—symbolic of the lost soul. For nine days she wanders, taking no food and no sweet nectar. At last she arrives at the Sacred Well, the Well of the Dances, the Kallichoron Well, at Eleusis.

There she was found by the king's four beautiful daughters who came to draw water from the well. Disguised as an old tired woman, Demeter was taken home with them to meet their mother, the queen. Queen Metanirs, pitying her, hired her to nurse her infant son—tiny prince Demophon. Demeter, desiring to bestow immortality upon the child, often immersed his form into the midst of flames which she had transformed into the essence of

Hades carrying off Persephone

white light. One night the queen, overcome with curiosity, beheld this ritual and, horrified, immediately dismissed Demeter as
nurse and sought to drive her from the palace. Whereupon Demeter dropped her disguise and revealed her true identity: *I am the
illustrious Demeter, who succors and comforts both mortals and
immortals. But hasten now and build me a great temple, and
beneath it an altar. Build it above the Kallichoron Well. After-
wards I myself will teach you the manner in which you shall
worship, and if you follow this with reverence, you shall be granted my favor.*

In a short time the Eleusinians had erected the first enormous
temple. From the temple Demeter seeks help from the sun, who
tells her Hades has taken Persephone to his kingdom beneath the
Earth and forced her to become his queen. In her grief, Demeter
withholds her blessings from the land and crops begin to fail. Only
with the approach of famine, does Zeus agree to help Demeter
free their daughter. He sends Hermes, messenger of the gods, to
persuade Hades to return Persephone to the upper regions. But
it is not possible to allow her to return full time because she has
eaten the seed of a pomegranate, the food of mortality and of the
dead, which obliges her to remain in the underworld for four
months of every year. So happy was Demeter to have her eight
months of the year, she restores fertility to the Earth.

This allegorical drama was performed in the Lesser Mysteries. It was accepted as depicting the succession of the seasons—
referring to the natural events of spring, summer, autumn and
winter. The populace conceived this as an interpretation of Persephone manifesting solar energy which lived underground with
Hades during the winter months, but who emerged in the summer
to restore Earth to fertility and productiveness. The drama depicted flowers and agriculture shrinking and dying of grief with
the departure of Persephone to the lower realms at the approach
of winter and coming to life again with her return to the regions
of light in the spring.

To the initiates of the Greater Mysteries, however, the allegory revealed its spiritual interpretation. Persephone symbolized the soul, which had been captured by the dark side of its nature and carried downward to incarnation in a physical form. The physical form in the Mysteries was recognized as a tomb, a lower aspect, an unreality, a sepulcher which held the soul prisoner in the lower kingdom of matter. The true home of the soul, however, was in the higher planes of spirit. And Persephone, as the soul, perpetually longed for a return to her spiritual freedom. During its sojourn in the physical form, the soul invariably became entangled in the desires of Earth—in a perpetual seeking after material possessions, represented by the pomegranate seed. The seekings and desires clouded its true perceptions and prevented its conscious assent toward seeking its spiritual nature.

The allegory also referred to reincarnation—with Persephone, the soul, spending part of the time in the lower world and part in the upper spiritual realms between births. She returned to the lower realms because desires drew her downward to reincarnation. The Greater Mysteries taught not only reincarnation but that though the soul was chained to the material world during its waking conscious hours it was released in liberation through sleep during the night hours to return to its travels on the upper planes. The initiates of the Greater Mysteries also recognized these activities as spiritual regeneration and liberation of higher consciousness from the bondage of material darkness.

In the secret rites of the Greater Mysteries, the Eleusinian initiates came to know that birth in the physical world was actually death to the higher worlds. But they also recognized that the physical form offered opportunity to unfold the immortal Self. The sojourn in the lower worlds of matter offered the soul the opportunity to overcome material desires and focus the greatest impact of consciousness toward liberation from the world of matter and the freedom of the higher spheres. The initiate knew that the majority were ruled by their lower animalistic personalities, while the rare light seeker used each physical incarnation as a stepping stone toward higher soul progression. Because the Greater Mysteries believed that the terrestrial world and the celestial world were in closest attunement at midnight, most of the Greater Mysteries were conducted at the midnight hour.

The secrets imparted at Eleusis have never been totally understood because each initiate took the vow of secrecy and swore on his life not to reveal them. Because they kept their vows so well, little is known today of the actual procedure. Thus the Mysteries have remained and forever will remain mysteries. Dire punishments and sometimes even death were imposed upon any who disclosed anything concerning the Mysteries. Alcibiades, famous playwright in Greece, is reported to have tried, after a dinner with friends, to mimic symbolic acts from the Mysteries, thereby desecrating them. He was charged with "impiety" and expelled from society. Aeschylus, the great dramatist, came very near to losing his life when an infuriated populace chased him out of the city because they believed that one of his tragedies revealed some of the secrets of the Mysteries. He was later exiled from Athens. Pausanias, a second century traveler, has given us precious information about the ancient world, but when he attempted to reveal the Mysteries of Eleusis, he had a dream. In the dream he was warned against such revelations, thus his descriptions of Eleusis stops at the entrance to the sanctuary. Strabo, too, a most prolific writer of antiquity, describes only the monuments he viewed outside the sanctuary.

Thus, through the centuries the Mysteries were preserved. The most famous people in antiquity were initiated into them. Even the peasantry among the populace were initiated into the Lesser Mysteries. In Roman times Emperors paid homage to Eleusis and some were initiated into the Mysteries.

Socrates was invited many times to become an initiate. He declined because the vows would seal his tongue. He wanted the freedom to teach and guide his disciples without restrictions. Furthermore, he was already well acquainted with the wisdom of how to unlock the inner powers of the soul. It was his possession of that wisdom and teachings that attracted such philosophers as Plato. During those days, Eleusis was called the sanctuary of the world. Even slaves were admitted to the Lesser Mysteries. The only qualification required was that a person not be guilty of murder.

Greek philosopher Themistius describes the secret of Eleusis thusly: *The soul, at the point of death, suffers the same feelings as those who are being initiated into the Greater Mysteries. First there are wanderings and weary, devious hurryings to and fro, journeyings incomplete and full of fears. Then before the end, every sort of terror, shudderings and tremblings, sweats and horrors. Then after that a marvelous sight meets you and pure regions of meadows receive you and there are voices, and dancing, and wonderful and holy sounds and sacred lights. And he that is completed and initiated wanders free and unrestrained and is crowned and joined in the worship among pure and holy men.*

Herodotus who, like Pythagoras, was initiated into the Egyptian and Cabiri Mysteries, was ever mindful of his vows of secrecy during his writings. He says: "Whoever has been initiated into the rites of Cabiri, this one understands what I am saying."

Proclus declared that initiation transformed the soul from a material, sensual, and purely human life to a communion and celestial intercourse with the gods. Purity of morals was required and elevation of the soul promised.

Aristophanes said:*We initiates alone are the only fortunate souls. It is upon us alone that the beneficent day star shineth. We alone receive pleasure from the influence of his rays.*

Cicero, the renowned philosopher, said: *It seems to me that Athens has produced nothing comparable to the Mysteries which, for a wild and ferocious life, have substituted humanity and urbanity of manners. It is through them that we, in reality, have learned the first principles of life—and they soften the pains of death by the hope of a better life hereafter.*

And again, Cicero: *Nothing is higher than these Mysteries. They have sweetened our characters and softened our customs. They have made us pass from the condition of savages to true humanity. They have not only shown us the way to live joyfully, but they have taught us how to die with a better hope.*

Of these secret Mysteries, Homer wrote: *Happy he of the mortals who has seen this. In the dark kingdom of shadows (in death), the fate of the initiate and the uninitiate is not the same. Those Mysteries of which no tongue can speak—only blessed is he whose eyes have seen them. His lot after death is not as the lot of other men.*

Plato wrote: *When a man dies, he experiences happenings like those who are initiated into the Mysteries. Our whole life is a journey by torturous ways without outlet. At the moment of quitting it, comes terrors, shuddering fear, amazement. Then a Light moves to meet you. Pure meadows receive you—songs and dances and Holy Apparitions.*

The Lesser Mysteries, which took place in the spring, the time of the vernal equinox, were available to a wide populace, but access to the Greater Mysteries could not be bought with either wealth or political influence. Only selected candidates could be initiated into the Greater Mysteries.

We do know the procession of initiation of the Lesser Mysteries began in Athens at a sanctuary called Agra near the Ilissos River. Agra was dedicated to Artemis. The procession started to perform in mid-February, the initiates for the procession gathering at Agra for purification and sacrifice in which the candidates were consecrated. Ceremonies of these consecrations and purifications prepared the Mystae to take part in the Greater Mysteries several months later in the year.

The Greater Mysteries were celebrated from mid-September to late October at the time of the autumnal equinox. Purification required the candidates for initiation to abstain from fish, beans, pomegranates and apples until after the festivities. The high priest was called the hierophant, as in the Egyptian Mysteries. S/he wore a purple cloak signifying royalty. Although the hierophant could be a married man or woman, s/he must remain chaste during the festival and initiatory ceremonies.

The Greater Mysteries began on the 14th of September. The pilgrims gathered first at Eleusis and from there set off in a great procession for Athens. The procession began at sunrise. Many stops along the Sacred Way—the name of the roadway—were made at temples where ritualistic singing, chanting and dancing occurred. Holy priests and priestesses marched in the procession and many of the populace fell on their knees to beg blessings and healings from the goddess Demeter as her statue was carried past them. As this great procession approached Athens it left the Sacred Way, crossed through the ancient Agora and finished at the Eleusinion in the city, a center which was regarded as an offshoot or extension of the sanctuary at Eleusis. There, the priests and priestesses deposited the sacred objects they had carried from Eleusis. The Eleusinion stood on the east side of the stone-paved Panathenaic Way between the rocks below the Propylaea of the Acropolis and the south side of the Stoa of Attalus.

The next day, the 15th of September, the hierophant called the populace of the city to the Agora, the market place. Before them he made the official proclamation of the opening of the festivities. He issued an invitation for everyone to participate except those guilty of murder or those who could not speak Greek. The initiates were dressed in pure white tunics. They were separated from the rest of the crowd. Before the hierophant, they knelt to receive the divine benediction. At sunrise on the morning of the 16th, heralds went through the city calling on the initiates to proceed to the sea for great purification baptisms.

On the 19th the great procession of initiates, together with the priests and priestesses, returned to Eleusis. This was the most splendid day of the festival. Led by the hierophant and followed by the initiates and then the populace, they set out on their procession. The hierophant carried a wooden image of the god Dionysus. The procession halted at all the sanctuaries along the Sacred Way—at Daphne, the sanctuary of the Daphneian Apollo; at the sanctuary of Aphrodite. Rituals were performed and prayers made to Apollo and Aphrodite. At the temple of Rhetoi a stop was made so that a saffron colored band could be attached to the right wrist and ankle of all pilgrims to protect against the evil eye. There the initiates chanted and performed sacred dances. Myrtle leaves were woven into the hair of the marchers. Each initiate carried a myrtle bough or a statue sacred to Dionysus.

The pilgrims arrived at Eleusis at dusk. The night procession began with the lighting of torches and dancing around the famous Well of the Beautiful Dances—the Kallichoron Well—where Demeter sat when she first arrived after her nine-day search for Persephone. Then the pilgrims wandered aimlessly along the shore with their flickering torches mimicking Demeter's search for Persephone.

At this point a division was made. The Mystae were separated from the Epoptes. The Mystae were told they must progress another year before they were eligible for initiation and must proceed through further purification disciplines. An initiate seeking higher initiations in the Greater Mysteries was never admitted until he or she had successfully graduated from the Lesser. The Epoptes were then guided into the inner temple, the Telesterion. At its entrance they were given the secret password which must be used at all the sacred temples from that day forward. The fast of the initiates was broken by drinking Kykion, a mystical drink from the soma plant, and partaking of cakes of sesame and wheat flour. What followed next is not clear since that is where the vow of secrecy occurred.

An Omphalos stone—much like that at Delphi—marked the entrance to the lower world through which the initiates descended, the place of death from which only the initiate might return to "live again." The site of the Omphalos was chosen because it marked a force center of extremely potent electromagnetic energies, rising up from the earth to meet downpouring ethers from celestial spheres. Like a cosmic crystal it acted as a type of obelisk embodying these forces. The "marriage" of these forces—the positive with the negative—caused the entire temple gridwork to reverberate with dynamic pranic ethers.

Thus each cave-temple site was carefully chosen because of these forces and the Omphalos stone marked it as a gridpoint of Greater initiations. There were such stones at Eleusis, Ephesus and Delphi.

During a part of the secret ceremonies, deep within the cave, a young infant representing Dionysus acted out a birth from a Virgin. Ringed by torches, this symbolic birth was carried out representing the birth of a new soul in fire—a burning away of the old self and the birth of the new out of the ashes.

At a crucial moment in the ceremony the hierophant announced "the mistress hath given birth to the holy boy," and Dionysus would appear in the form of a babe, surrounded by torches of brilliant mysterious white light, signifying transformation of the soul and the birth of the soul into a new life, again burning away the old self, and the birth arising from the ashes of the old. The cave was filled with enchanting sights and sounds, songs, dances—and there the Epoptae fell into a trance and communed directly with the gods through heavenly visions. Many experienced out-of-body contacts with the gods and goddesses.

Finally the gates of the adytum were thrown open and a great light burst out of the darkness of the cave with the awesome sounds of a mammoth drum. In the midst of the blinding light there appeared Persephone in an epiphany (or divine appearance).

It is evident that strict secrecy hid a miraculous happening in the Eleusinian Mysteries connected in a mysterious way to a great cosmic event—perhaps the coming of the space gods to Earth. Otherwise the fascination with these Mysteries could not have continued for so many centuries. The sacrifices, the labyrinthian journey from Athens, the terrors of the underworld, the drama of the birth of Dionysus from white light and the dramatic return of the beloved Persephone from the underworld, created within both observers and initiate a philosophical transformation with which nothing else could have so vividly compared.

It is known that the blindfolded candidates were conducted on an obstacle course—a labyrinth—around the vast inner temple, accompanied by a tremendous storm, thunder peals and lightning. They were caused to traverse perilous streams of water. They realized they had entered a cave of stupendous magnitude and beauty. They were shown successive scenes of darkness and light, terror and awe. Female candidates were known to faint. With the removal of the blindfold they were told: *You have seen what I passed through, yet I rose again and so will you. Here is the initiate's secret. That death is a passage and no more.*

In other words, they were persuaded that death is only the passage to a better life. Every effort was made to remove the fear of death from the consciousness of the initiate. The moment the light was shown to him, he witnessed the brilliant spaces of Elysium—the far-reaching meadows, the breathtaking skies, the heavenly voices, the glories of another world. We do know that during their trance state, many initiates in an out-of-body experience came "face to face" with the gods and goddesses of Mt. Olympus.

Throughout the nine days of initiation, with each passing day the neophyte experienced ever increasing brilliancy as s/he attained growth of the consciousness from the lower state to the state of supreme illumination—the Place of Light. Following the soul-stirring initiatory ceremony in the great cave, on the ninth day the new initiates were escorted into a secret room where they stood before a magnificent statue of the goddess Demeter surrounded by all the hierophants and Ptahs in their robes and hoods. There they were instructed in the highest of the secrets. Only after completing this final ceremony was the initiate recognized as an Epoptes, the highest initiate. After this climax the initiates gathered in a nearby meadow. There they chanted and feasted, releasing the tension created by anticipation of the days before.

During initiation in Egypt each candidate was first directed downward into the pits of the lower world which symbolized his birth into matter. Struggling there with the concepts of his own thought forces and thoughtforms and overcoming them, he was then led slowly upward toward increasingly lighted rooms and more beautiful robes, to finally emerge in the king's chamber to undergo his final initiation. There is little doubt that the Eleusinian ceremonies mimicked the Mysteries of Egypt.

Eleusis Today

Immense broken pillars lie everywhere, many still displaying their ancient lettering. Fragments of immense stone stairways lead up a tree-covered hill which sits behind the remains of the vast temple, carved into the rock, with its facade facing the east, as if waiting to greet the early morning sun.

The Eleusinian Mysteries were in force during the time of Jesus and survived at least four hundred years after his death. Like Ephesus, they were finally suppressed in the seventh century by Theodosius who slaughtered all who refused to accept Christianity.

Surrounding the town now are many industries—soap, turpentine, spirits, building material and cement are among its industrial products. If one seeks with discernment, one great cave of initiation remains. The cave entrance is beautifully arched. The presence of the cave and its electromagnetic forces are what induced the Builders to construct a statue for Demeter on these holy grounds. The cave offered an excellent area for the secrets of the Greater Mysteries to be revealed. Eleusis was a meeting place of the initiates who gathered to share the secrets of the Mysteries and experience additional training toward further initiations.

The name Eleusis comes from the verb "Elauno," meaning "I come," from the coming of Demeter to the Well and referring to the great temple built for her in which she sought refuge in her grief at the loss of her beloved daughter Persephone. It was also given the name Eleusis after the hero Eleusis, the son of Hermes. His son was Celeus, the first king of the small city kingdoms in that region and the original founder of the first kingdom of Eleusis.

During the time when Solon, the great lawgiver of Athens, was in control, the sanctuary at Eleusis grew beyond belief. When Pericles came to power in the mid-fifth century B.C. he further expanded the sanctuary, repairing and transforming it into an international center for worship. Light seekers the world over visited Greece seeking participation in the Eleusinian Mysteries.

When Rome conquered Athens, Eleusis fell somewhat in grandeur but still maintained a place of reverence and respect. When Julian became emperor he made an attempt to reestablish some of the glory of Eleusis. But he was murdered for his efforts.

When Valentinian ascended to power he issued an edict demanding that there be no more nocturnal rituals, meaning initiatory rites. He made one exception—that of the rites of Eleusis—because the Greek populace issued such a cry of despair he realized for the first time the tremendous importance of this religious center. However, when Alaric invaded Greece only thirty-two years after Emperor Valentinian, he totally destroyed the Mystery School—which was, in reality, destroying a place where God and man joined hands. The Greater Mysteries of Eleusis enabled the initiate to rise out of his waking conscious level to greet the inner deity. But the new Christians, viewing them only as pagan orgies, and failing to discern their truth, closed the door to initiation for untold centuries. They took, however, their secret documents and threaded their light into the dogmas of their own expanding faith.

There still remains the sacred Well 'round which the initiates performed ritual dances. There is a small walled-in terrace which was once the Sanctuary of Hades. The carved seats of the gigantic temple now lie in ruin, still reflecting their past story. The cave which remains was once the entrance to the mammoth cavern into which the Epoptae descended for the secret rites of the Greater initiation. The entrance has now been carefully sealed.

When personally exploring the site, I longed to enter the sealed up cave. Perhaps old memories may have stirred, resurrecting the glory of an initiation my soul experienced here in the long ago, the dear dead days now beyond recall. But standing among those ruins, with the surrounding factories, smoke stacks and dreariness of the nearby dingy little village pressing in upon me, it was hard to imagine I had once stood there, beholding the unearthly light which burst forth around the virgin Persephone, or to bring to remembrance the rapture of the soul I once was. It wasn't like it was at Delphi, with its breathtaking surroundings and grandeur. It was easier to walk away and pretend the past had never been. But pausing to look back, I glimpsed a vision through a long tube of memories, and, reaching through the mists of time, I touched the face of God.

The power and majesty of this site is still strong though the temple was destroyed over 1600 years ago. The currents of energy established here still rise like obelisks upreaching to meet downflowing airwaves. It is still a holy site.

The cave that once opened to an underground temple of initiation is now sealed. It was here we buried a crystal, near the Omphalos stone, and linked Eleusis to all the sacred sites of initiation throughout the world.

Although the light of the great Mystery School at Eleusis now seems extinguished, modern mystics are aware that it is merely sleeping. The voices of thousands of its initiates call from the cave of initiation across the centuries to those who seek the light as it is reborn in the new age of today.

Chapter Ten

The Dionysian Mysteries

In the Dionysian cult the grape symbolized the source of human salvation, since its life essence, the juice, symbolized the blood of the deity. In the drama itself the god Dionysus always appears with grapes interwoven in his hair and the vine of the grapes winding about his physical form. In the light of esoteric teachings, we immediately recognize this significant symbology. We concede the grapes themselves to represent the concentrated Christ Substance,* (celestial ethers) or "the blood of the deity," concentrated in the oversoul above the head of man. And we recognize the vine to symbolize the antahkarana or the mystic etheric thread connecting the divine Self with the lower personality.

The cluster of grapes entwined in Dionysus' hair symbolizes the Christ Substance penetrating the brain and permeating the entire human form via the vine, or the divine thread, which ultimately diffuses the bloodstream. Thus in modern days when

---

*See Astara's *Book of Life,* the hidden teachings of the degrees, available only to Astarians. For information write Astara, 800 W. Arrow Hwy. P.O. Box 5003, Upland, CA 91785-5003.

Christians, taking holy communion, drink the juice of the grape in remembrance of the Christ, they are symbolically partaking of a portion of the Christ Substance (divine atmospheric akasha) to purify the physical bloodstream.

In the rites performed in the Dionysian Mysteries, the initiate, actually partaking of the Christ Substance through spiritual ecstasy, was "saved by the blood of Christ" or changed by the purification of the physical bloodstream through the entrance of the Christ Substance pouring down through the antahkarana, or the vine, into his or her own personal bloodstream, destroying thereby the karmic picture images which had bound him/her to the wheel of destiny and rebirth.*

Thus in the true Dionysian Mysteries, the intoxicating effect of wine played no part whatever in the sacred teachings. Sad to say, the Romans converted the Dionysian Mysteries of the Greeks into the Mysteries of Bacchus, where those partaking understood little of the true wine of salvation and, partaking of the physical, material wine, became nothing more than intoxicated individuals indulging in drunken orgies called the Bacchanalia. The true meaning of the Dionysian Mysteries became lost in the deplorable exoteric display of excessive wine and lust.

The Inner Teachings

In the Dionysian drama, as in all the other Mysteries, first to be established was the existence of the Ineffable Cause, representing the divine Godhead, the Supreme Manifestation. Within this Ineffable Cause existed Ether and Chaos. Ether represented the masculine manifestation of spirit and Chaos the feminine aspect of matter—positive and negative attributes of divinity. In the drama, the union of these two gave birth to another sphere of existence which they called "the Cosmic Egg." This was the divine son or the plane of the Christ Substance. The Orphic Egg

*Again, see *Book of Life*.

From Thomassin's Collection

The Processional of the Bacchic Rites
When the populace, denied entry into the Greater Mysteries, imbibed the wine of the Holy Eucharist, the sacred procession of the mystics who sought initiation in the Eleusinian Mysteries became a procession of Bacchic debauchery.

symbolized this estate—that of a divine etheric substance which, entering the consciousness of the initiate, caused a sublime ecstasy. This was the true wine, of which the grapes were only a crude symbol.

To repeat, the Orphic Egg was symbolized by a mammoth egg with the body of a serpent entwining it, with its tail at the bottom of the egg and the upraised head at the top—depicting the awakened serpent power of kundalini which was the sure means of establishing spiritual ecstasy. Pouring down from the plane of Christ Substance to manifest on a lower level was the plane of universal mind called "Phanes."

Out of the plane of Phanes poured the great sea of maya—the Mother Substance, the mother of creation, mother night, the plane of the celestial waters. *In the beginning God created the heavens and the Earth and the Earth was without form and void. And the spirit of God moved upon the face of the waters and God said, "Let there be light."* Phanes, the spirit of God, moving upon the face of the waters, the great mother maya, brings forth the celestial firmament, the heaven plane, which, in the Mystery drama, was called Uranus. Bringing forth a second "son," they produced the planet Earth and all the other stars and worlds which form our sidereal kingdom.

Another effect of the universal consciousness moving upon mother night produced a son called Saturn or Time, possessing all the limitations imposed by time upon matter and upon mortals. Saturn, the forces of Time, waged war against Uranus, the forces of heaven or space, and overcame him, thereby making Saturn— or Time—the ruler of the lower worlds. Time became superior to space.

Saturn took unto himself a wife, the goddess Rhea, queen of the world of matter or material Space. Out of this union—between the god of Time and the goddess of Space—are born two divine children, a son and a daughter: Zeus, god of the sidereal firmament, and Hera, his twin sister, goddess of the sidereal firmament.

The union of Saturn with Rhea (Time and Space) created many other children. Saturn turns upon his children and devours them, which is to say that Time obscures and destroys all things— things existing in the world of matter or limited space. But Rhea, his queen, rescues her infant son, Zeus, from Saturn and hides him away. Zeus, growing to maturity, attacks his father, Saturn, and overcomes him, thus becoming the ruler of the material worlds—which is to say that Zeus represents a method of overcoming Time and Space, a method not manifest to those dwelling in three dimensions. Zeus is god of the fourth dimension.

Zeus, having ascended the universal throne to become the ruler of heaven and Earth, desires to wed Rhea, his own mother—that is, he wishes to bring into the space of the third dimension an understanding of the fourth dimension—a knowledge of how to overcome Time and Space.

From their union the goddess Demeter is born, goddess of agriculture in the third dimension. Uniting with Zeus through immaculate conception Demeter gives birth to their daughter Persephone. When Persephone unfolds into fair maidenhood she, as a divine Virgin, impregnated by Zeus, the Holy Spirit of the Christ Substance, brings forth Zeus' divine son, Dionysus, again through immaculate conception. The union of Zeus with Persephone is a Mystery drama unto itself—the union of the fourth dimension with the zodiacal sign of the Virgin. Thus Dionysus, born of this union, came to Earth from a dimension higher than Time and Space, through the manifestation of an astrological sign of the Virgin, manifesting aspects of both the divine masculine and the divine feminine. Dionysus was to the initiates of the Mysteries what Jesus is to us mystic Christians—a manifestation of God-made-man.

Dionysus, beautiful and divine son of Zeus, was a constant delight to his father. Zeus even placed him on his own throne and allowed the child to amuse himself by playing with the great scepter that ruled the lower kingdoms. Zeus taught his tiny son how to control the elements of the lower worlds, using the power of lightning and the thunderbolts as playthings.

Now, in the sidereal kingdom was the planet Earth, upon which had appeared the race of the Titans. The Titans were possibly visitors from other planets who had journeyed to Earth as did the gods and goddesses of Olympus. Or they were the result of the efforts of genetic engineering on the part of a race of beings who came long before the Olympians arrived. They were called the offspring of Cronus and Gaea, so they could be the children of an earlier race of visitors who attempted to unite space gods with Earth primitives. Certainly the race of the monstrous giants were such, as well as the Cyclopes. It was the Titans who perpetually sought to gain power over Zeus and the other gods when they arrived to inhabit Earth.

Hera, the twin sister of Zeus and his legitimate wife, who, within her divine right was the feminine controller of the mundane spheres, watched with extreme jealousy the developing power of the child Dionysus. Beholding how favored he was in his father's sight, she sought some way to bring about his destruction. In desperation, she turned to the Titans for help. The Titans, equally desiring to overthrow the power of the divine Dionysus, joined with Hera in a plan to destroy him.

The six-year-old child spent most of his time playing in the spheres of his father's universe. His traditional playthings were called, in the Mystery drama, "winged wheels, a spinning top, the Golden Apples from the Hesperides, a Golden Fleece, a ball and a pair of dice."

Hera, observing the habits of Dionysus, devised a scheme to lead the young child far away from the watchful eye of his father, Zeus. Since she was queen of the world of illusions, it was not difficult for her, with the help of the Titans, to gather the substance of maya and create a mirror of illusion into which would be reflected the image of the entire dimensions of the lower worlds. The mirror would also reflect the face of anyone looking into it.

Dionysus, finding the mirror of illusion among his playthings in the world of space and gazing into it, saw in it not only his own form and face but the reflection of all of the lower spaces. Gazing upon the image of a fair child, the young god, believing him to be a desirable playmate, immediately sought to grasp the reflected image. The Titans, observing that Dionysus had fallen victim to their scheme, moved the mirror of illusion farther and farther away and Dionysus, following after it, was drawn deep into the heart of the lower regions.

Having enmeshed him in the field of illusion, the Titans fell upon the divine child to destroy him. Young Dionysus, becoming aware of his danger and, possessing great powers because of his divinity, sought many ways of escape by changing himself into many forms. First he became a lion, then a horse, then a horned snake, a tiger, and finally, a bull. Even with his divine powers, however, he was not able to escape the Titans, and in the form of the bull he was finally slain.

The Titans, having succeeded in slaying the young god, were at once faced with the problem of how to hide their crime from the all-seeing eye of his watchful father, Zeus. They decided to dismember his body in the form of a bull, to broil the dismembered parts over a fire and devour them so that Zeus might never detect their atrocity.

But Zeus, becoming aware of the absence of his son, discovered the Titans devouring his body. He hastily dispatched the goddess Athena to rescue the heart of Dionysus before the Titans could consume it. Athena, swooping down from the higher realms, rescued the heart of the divine child and delivered it to Zeus. Then Zeus, hurling great thunderbolts, struck down the Titans and utterly destroyed them with fire. The ashes of the Titans, however, since they had devoured the form of the god, contained not only their own animalistic Titanic properties but the divine flesh and blood of the god who, in this drama, represents the Christ Substance. Out of these ashes containing both lower matter and divinity, Zeus created the human race, because he realized these beings, possessing portions of his beloved son Dionysus, would eventually overcome their Titanic heritage and express divinity.

The divine heart of Dionysus, however, was reclaimed by Zeus who, saddened by his great loss, set out to search through all the races to find another consort worthy to mother a rebirth of Dionysus. In his searching among humanity, Zeus discovered a fair maiden named Europa and abducted her. Her father, Agenor, discovering her absence, dispatched his son, Cadmus, to find her. He admonished Cadmus not to return home without his sister on pain of death.

Cadmus searched diligently for Europa but could not discover her whereabouts and, realizing that his cause was hopeless and that he could never return again to his father's house, consulted an oracle as to his future course of action. The oracle instructed Cadmus to search until he discovered a cow and then to follow the cow until it stopped. On the place where the cow stopped he was to build a city and call it Thebes. Cadmus followed the instructions. After building the city called Thebes, Cadmus fell in love with a maiden named Harmonia, who possessed great virtue, and they were wed.

From the marriage of Cadmus and Harmonia five children were born. The first of these five children was a most beautiful daughter called Semele. Semele was perfection personified. Her beauty was incomparable, and she was completely devoted to the attainment of divinity and to the service of God. She entered the temples as a Temple Virgin, and it was there that Zeus found her. Beholding her, Zeus realized that here was the consort for whom he had searched. Here was one worthy to mother the rebirth of Dionysus. Taking the cherished heart of the divine infant, he ground it into a fine powder, placed it in a bottle of wine and sent it to Semele. Semele consumed this divine potion. Thus Dionysus was immaculately conceived.

But Hera was ever watchful for the rebirth of Dionysus. Observing that Semele had conceived and was to bring forth a child, Hera assumed the form of Semele's old nurse named Beroe. In the guise of the gentle old nurse, Hera-Beroe began to plant doubts in the mind of Semele as to the true divinity of the father of her coming child. Semele had never beheld Zeus except as he appeared to her in mortal form. Hera persuaded Semele that if Zeus really were divine, he should prove his divinity by appearing to her garbed in his immortal Olympian glory.

Semele approached Zeus and asked for proof of his divinity. Zeus, loving Semele well, promised to prove his divinity to her in any manner she could devise. Semele then asked that he appear to her in his immortal form in all its splendor. Zeus, realizing his tragic mistake in promising to satisfy her whims, and realizing Hera had inspired her request knowing it would destroy Semele, implored her not to insist upon this favor. He knew too that, being mortal, Semele would be destroyed by his radiance. But Semele was adamant.

Zeus, bound by his promise, had no choice but to don his robes of power and descend to Semele arrayed in all his god-glory. As Zeus descended, the city where Semele dwelt, unable to withstand the resplendent divine fires with which Zeus was surrounded, burst into flames, including the house where Semele lived. Zeus, beholding her burning home, immediately covered the house with grapes and ivy leaves, protecting it from complete destruction. Then, searching among the ashes for his beloved Semele, Zeus discovered her burned body and took from it the still living form of his yet unborn son, Dionysus. The soul of the beautiful Semele descended to the regions of Hades.

Zeus carried Dionysus back to the heaven realms and, creating an artificial womb in his own side, placed Dionysus therein, where he was to remain for the last two months of gestation. Upon completion of this period Dionysus was reborn from the side of his father, Zeus. Zeus, desiring to remove him from Hera's wrath, and resolving that *this* twice-born infant son would receive the finest spiritual education, gave him into the keeping of Hermes, who took the infant far away from Mount Olympus to the garden of Nysa in Arabia. Here Dionysus spent his childhood and here, under the especially watchful eye of Silenus, the most learned of the satyrs, he grew into magnificent maturity. On attaining maturity, Dionysus descended into the regions of Hades, found his beloved mother Semele and, carrying her into the heaven world, placed her among the immortals.

Returning to Earth he spent his life in spreading the doctrines of the Mysteries—the teachings of the immortality and the divinity of man. When he had completed his mission on Earth, Dionysus ascended at last to the heaven realm to dwell with his father Zeus with whom, after so many wanderings, he was reunited forever.

While on Earth, Dionysus traveled throughout the world teaching the Dionysian Mysteries and initiation. His teachings were cherished everywhere except in his own country. But was not the same true of Jesus? Although the people would have welcomed him home, the state opposed him and his teachings. Unfortunately, the Dionysian rites could be accepted from two different viewpoints. First, the populace, unprepared to receive the awakening of higher consciousness, debased through ignorance many of the sacred ceremonies. Not understanding the true meaning of the initiation, they turned to ritualistic orgies, causing the concept, whose real and primary purpose was to stress the blessings of cosmic consciousness, the joy of life and the freedom of thought to become debased through their misunderstanding.

Long after Dionysus left the Earth plane, those too ignorant to perceive the true meaning were responsible for a misinterpretation of the actual rites, so that every action, every form and ritual was twisted into a semblance of debauchery and wickedness. Thus the Bacchanalian doctrine met the opposition of the state. Eventually, debauchery did spring into the ill-famed Bacchanalia. A wild festival was held in the name of Dionysus and practiced under his banner. Responding to the effects of wine and intoxicating liquors, the Bacchanalia degenerated into scenes of demoralized practices and, in their gatherings, were instituted plots and intrigues against the government—until it became necessary to capture and punish the members of the Bacchanalia. These souls brought down the high estate of Dionysus, causing him to be defamed throughout history.

This is, in brevity, the drama of the Dionysian Mysteries. We have just given you the exoteric description of the drama as it was portrayed in the Lesser Mysteries. But what is the inner esoteric explanation of this involved drama? What does it mean to initiates in the light of our esoteric teachings? How does it teach of the divine Christ Substance, of the true Eucharist, and of its true purpose in our lives?

The "Sacrifice" of the Sun God and the Planetary God

It is extremely difficult for the human mind with its limited powers of concept to understand the imprisonment of a solar god actually within the confines of the sun of our solar system and of the tremendous sacrifice imposed by this voluntary imprisonment.

We are concerned here with a cosmic mystery and it is not expected that the reaches of the ordinary mind can understand and appreciate the inner workings of these cosmic planetary forces. Thus the reason for the Lesser and Greater Mysteries. The Greater secrets were concealed from the profane—because it would be pointless and even dangerous to prostitute such sublime truths and sciences by exposing them to the populace incapable of understanding them. As well teach the theory of divine physics to an infant. Even many of the initiates failed to grasp the whole meaning of their initiation.

Suffice to say the solar god himself is not so imprisoned in the body of our sun, but the emanations of his astral body are and he must, because of this, confine his cosmic activities principally to the regions of our solar system and especially the planet Earth. He has thus limited his cosmic activities for many eons to come until the lifestream of this planet can lift itself out of its degrading karma and enter its state of blessedness.

His sacrifice was made at intense suffering beyond the power of our understanding. Suffice to say it is the purpose of the Divine Hierarchy to help lift our humanity toward the heights of its potential godhood so that the solar god may once again gain his liberation. This will not transpire for many ages to come. However, this does not release each individual disciple and initiate from his or her duty to do his utmost to perpetuate the purposes of the Hierarchy by so living a life that will aid and abet these eminent purposes.

Needless to say, there is an equal mystery in the ensouling of the great cosmic goddess who inhabits Mother Earth, our planet. Recognized as a planetary goddess, she too has ensouled the planet with her astral being and is equally confined to this planet for eons to come. This cosmic Mother is symbolized by all the great Earth goddesses—Athena, Demeter, Isis, Astarte, Ceres—even the Virgin Mary. As this lifewave evolves through our dark night of the soul, the suffering of Earth's planetary goddess is intense, and she has been forced several times in the past to eliminate the lifewave except for a few advanced souls as both the planet and its lifewave reach certain cosmic transitions. Such a transition—a Cosmic Judgment—faces our lifewave even now and, because we have almost totally destroyed our planet, the cosmic entity ensouling her may be forced once again to cause planetary destruction, possibly a pole shift.

Only the highest initiate is truly capable of understanding the sacrifice of a solar and a planetary god. Only the secrets of initiation could unveil the mystery.

The Mysteries According to the Solar Drama

Worship of the sun was expressed by humankind since the earliest beginnings of time and mankind on this planet—the Egyptians, the Mayans, the Aztecs, the Incas, the Greeks, the Indians, the Zoroastrians. But the primitive mind of early man understood sun worship far more than we moderns today. The gods had claimed to be direct descendants of the sun. They explained that the sun was like a great central planet of the solar system.

Its surface was not aflame with fire as Eartheans had supposed. They stated that in the atmospheric ethers existing between the sun and its planets there existed a ring of cosmic fire around the sun. The fire was constantly erupted by the influence of energy rays pouring from the sun to ignite the ring of fire. The beings dwelling on the various planets, beholding the fire, the flames, the heat, the light, supposed they came from the sun's surface. But they came from the celestial atmospheric ring of fire, many light years from the sun itself, but surrounding the sun.

There is a race of very special beings dwelling on the sun's surface—special because the sun *is* a very sacred planet or star. Those descending to Earth from the sun were called solar deities, or sun gods. The gods explained that the sun itself reflects light from the Great Central Sun, just as our moon reflects light from our sun. The gods further explained the involvement of a supreme cosmic deity in the actual body of the sun. They explained the sacrifice of the solar deity. They called him the Logos.

The primitives believed—because the gods had so taught them—that lifeforce was propelled to Earth through the rays of the sun's ring of fire because of the great deity's sacrifice. They were taught far beyond the idea that the sun nourished the earth; far beyond the activities of the elements in producing the substances necessary for humanity's bodily existence. To them the sun also represented the cause of all generation, the cause of the cosmic activities of the Absolute and the necessity of the solar deity's sacrifice in order that the lifewave might express through form. It was his creative energy that caused the evolution of both mortals and planet. Albert Pike, famed Masonic mystic, explained the worship of the sun thusly: *He was to them immense, indivisible, imperishable and everywhere present. It was their need of light and of his creative energy that was felt by all men and nothing was more fearful to them than his absence. His beneficent influences caused his identification with the principle of good and the Brahma of the Hindus, the Mithras of the Persians, Atum Amun Ptah and Osiris of the Egyptians, Bel of the Chaldeans, Adonai of the Phoenicians, Adonis and Apollo of the*

Greeks, became but personifications of the sun, the regenerating
principle, image of that fecundity which perpetuates and rejuve-
nates the world's existence.

There is no question that before the Great Pyramid of Egypt
reached its final stages it functioned as an astrological observa-
tory. So did some of the pyramids of Yucatan, especially Chich-
en Itza and Palenque. The massive monuments of stone, such as
Stonehenge in Britain, the Gate of the Sun at Tiahuanaca, the
Temples of the Sun at Copan, and other stone monuments were
all built not only as initiatory temples, but as astronomical obser-
vatories. The Builders of all these monuments throughout the
ages and throughout the planet were well versed in astronomy
and astrology—because most of them were built directly or indirectly under the auspices of the gods who visited Earth in those
early days. Indeed, the early religion of the race included knowledge of and reverence for the heavenly bodies. And the celestial
bodies were often named after the gods who visited Earth.

The fixed stars were shaped into specific constellations
through which the solar systems followed their pathway, and the
Dionysian Artificers or Initiate-Builders of Earth built their temples, their pyramids, their cathedrals to follow the formations of
the Great Architect of the Universe, the solar deity of this solar
system. They discerned that planet Earth is an immense magnetic
crystal, possessing a planned grid. They built their monuments
on the nodes of this gridwork the better to align the meridians
flowing between the monuments. Each monument on its particular node was so constructed as to call down cosmic ethers to further enhance its electromagnetic and cosmic properties.

The ancients were taught that the sun was worthy of worship,
but it only symbolized the supreme authority of the cosmic Creator. Out of cosmic astronomy evolved the concept of the Holy
Trinity. In all the Mystery Schools the creator was divided into
three aspects. Today, Masonry—a modern Mystery School—still
symbolizes the deity by an equilateral triangle. The sun, traveling through the pathway of the zodiac, assumed the nature of the
animal through whose house he was currently passing. To repeat,

since Taurus was represented by the sign of the bull, the sun was worshiped as a white bull by the Egyptians. He was given the name of Apis. Their worshiped god was called Serapis. The Assyrians named the sun Bel, Baal, or Bul during the sign of Taurus the Bull. When the sun passed into the sign of Leo the Lion, the lion became the symbol of the sun. In Pisces, the sun assumed the sign of the fish—Vishnu appearing as the fish god to the Hindus.

The ancients understood well that these animalistic signs and the gods who represented them were in every case the divine light, the solar deity personified. During the sign of Leo, Egyptian priests wore the skins of lions and the Ptah often wore the head-dress of the lion, symbolizing the personified divine light.

Hercules, the greatest hero of Greek mythology, was the personification of the solar deity. As he followed the pathway of his Twelve Labors he represented the sun traversing the twelve houses of the zodiac. His Twelve Labors symbolized benevolent activities bestowed upon the human race through the solar deity. After he slew the lion of Cithaeron, the Thespian lion, he wore its skin as a cloak. Often too he wore the headdress of the lion to symbolize the sun in Leo, just as the Ptahs in the Mystery Schools often wore the head mask of the lion during ceremonies of initiation.

The Greeks associated many of their gods and heroes with the being who ensouled the sun of our solar system—Dionysus, Apollo, Hercules, Hermes, Ulysses, Zeus, were all endowed with attributes of the sun, making them sun gods. The Norwegians worshiped Odin and his son Balder the Beautiful as solar deities— Odin because of his one eye, which they felt symbolized the sun. The Egyptians regarded Ra, Amun, Osiris and Hermes as sun gods, or souls who possessed the attributes of the solar deity. Isis was called the mother of the sun, or the Mother of God, since the sun symbolized God. The initiates of both Egypt and Greece understood that these divine beings actually came to Earth from the sun itself.

The Masons place their Worshipful Master on a throne in the East where the sun rises. The Worshipful Master thus represents the solar deity in physical form. As the sun bestows light and lifeforce upon the Earth and upon the human race, so is the Worshipful Master expected to bestow wisdom upon the Brothers of the Lodge.

The hierophants of the Mysteries wore garments embellished with the insignia of the solar orb with its rays flowing outward. Priests of the Catholic Church even today often wear garments embroidered with such insignia, but they have long since lost the meaning of the symbol.

The Mystery Schools of antiquity often portrayed the sun god as a beautiful blue-eyed youth with golden hair falling upon his shoulders. He often carried a lamb in his arms, symbolizing the vernal equinox, or the Ram in the sign of the zodiac. When the Catholic fathers came upon this symbol they bestowed the title of the Lamb of God upon Jesus and frequently portrayed him carrying a lamb in his arms—much like the sun god from the Mysteries, except that Jesus was portrayed as a shepherd saving a lost lamb, the lamb symbolizing the lost of humanity. Those who thus address him today as the Lamb of God fail to realize that the title refers to the Ram in the sign of the zodiac.

The Mysteries related truths concerning man the microcosm and God the Macrocosm. That which was related to God was called the *Solar Drama*, or the Macrocosmic Drama, and was portrayed according to the science of the zodiac as related to the sun god. That which was related to man was called the *Soular Drama*, or the Microcosmic Drama, and portrayed the individual soul traversing the path of life and, through initiation, attaining godhood.

According to the Solar Drama, the Mystery of the sun god, we have first the plane of divinity, the Godhead, in which the masculine Father principle moves upon the face of the Waters, the feminine Mother principle, out of which union comes their divine son, the plane of the Christ Substance which in the Ancient Wisdom was called the Monadic Plane. From the Monadic Plane are rayed divine emanations, out of which are created all of the worlds—the archetypal, the mental, the sidereal and the elemental kingdoms. Out of the stars of the sidereal kingdom are projected the four elements and from the four elements come the corporeal world. The corporeal world is the world of matter as opposed to the world of spiritual substance.

The world of the human kingdom, the animal kingdom, the plant kingdom, the mineral kingdom and the world of the elements reproduce themselves according to their kind. But from the heart of the substance out of which they come lies the Christ Substance, the root substance, vitalizing every atom. Without the vitalizing principle existing in the heart of the atom, nothing generates its kind. The sperm in the father cannot reproduce if the vitalizing quality is missing. The ovum-egg in the mother is void of reproductive possibilities if the vitalizing essence is absent. Nothing can come into being except that it be diffused by the divine Christ Substance or root substance which brings forth all manifestation. Thus, everything in the universe manifests with the one root substance at its base, but the divinity or Christ in humans remains unmanifested until it is activated into being by the creative activities of humans themselves.

The Father principle reigns as divine Fire; the Mother as the Holy Ghost or divine Water, Chaos. Their son, the Christ realm, reigns as the world of air or Ether. The heavens, with all their planes and spheres, came forth out of divine Fire—the Earth out of divine Water, the Mother. Mediating between the Fire and the Water is the divine son, the realm of Ether.

In the Dionysian drama the Father principle was named "Zeus," and the Mother principle "Demeter." Zeus represents the supreme masculine force manifesting in the lower created worlds. Demeter represents the supreme feminine force manifesting in the lower worlds. Their offspring, the feminine Persephone, represents the soul immersed in the mortal body—spending a period of time in the heavenly regions, then descending again to the world of matter to take on another Earthly personality, going back and forth between the two.

Zeus, as the Holy Spirit impregnating the Virgin Persephone, creates the birth of his divine son, Dionysus. In the cosmic drama Dionysus represents the Christ or the Christ Substance. The Christ Substance becomes, then, the "only begotten Son of God" and, from the plane of the Christ, the son's divine Substance, containing both the feminine and masculine attributes, rays down through all space the various emanations which, acting upon each other, produce the lower worlds and the lower kingdoms. Zeus thus becomes the father of Dionysus and simultaneously the father of the lower worlds, having produced them all out of himself. Dionysus, the Christ Substance, uses the sun of our solar system as his principal source of entrance into the atmosphere of the lower worlds. Thus Dionysus becomes the sun god, the solar deity, through whom the spiritual essences pour down upon the planets and people of the world of matter.

The Titans of Hesiod were twelve in number and were called the twelve governors of the world. In the Solar Drama, they represent the twelve planets in the celestial zodiac. The Titans, even though they are diffused and involved intricately in the material world, are also celestial for they are connected by etheric umbilical cords to the heart of the sun, representative of the Christ plane. The planets are connected not only by etheric cords to the sun itself, but are also connected one to the other. As certain planets pass through certain constellations, different cosmic activities are produced according to a planetary scheme called the science of the zodiac. The planets do influence each other and all of humanity existing upon the planets through the etheric connections established between them.

It is the twelve governors or twelve planets which, seizing upon Dionysus, distribute his "body," or the Christ Substance, the divine Ethers, among the lower worlds and give to all individual humans a portion of his divine form. But the heart of Dionysus is rescued by Zeus, which act prevents the Dionysian divine essence from being completely destroyed by the elements of the lower worlds.

Zeus, the Father principle in the Godhead, destroying the Titans or the twelve governors, represents the battle between spirit and matter, with spirit ultimately slaying matter and overcoming it, thereby releasing the imprisoned Christ Splendor in each being and in every atom. It rises out of the lower realms of matter and is resurrected back into its divine form. Thus the race is ultimately resurrected out of mortality into immortality, raising the Christ Substance within itself to its divine estate, overcoming the body and overcoming death.

Dionysus represents the plane or Substance which contains both the divine bread of life and the everlasting waters of eternal life. It is this divine Essence which the initiates of the Dionysian Mysteries were consuming when they "ate the body" and "drank the blood" of the sun god or the solar deity.

Each soul, consisting of both a lower Titanic nature and a higher Dionysian immortal nature, is capable of overcoming the Titanic within itself, of burning away these animalistic principles and bringing forth from the ashes the divine Essence, which is the Christ, within itself. The Soul is capable of transmuting its mortal body into an immortal one and overcoming the last enemy, death. The transmuted heart chakra becomes the heart of the divine Dionysus and the center of the immortal soul or the laboratory of transmutation, wherein the soul may become immortal.

The Dionysian Mysteries According to the Individual Soul

In the Soular Drama, the personal drama of the individual initiate, Zeus and Demeter become the divine monad in the auric egg of the soul. The divine monad possesses both the feminine and masculine attributes of divinity. Extending down into the physical form, Zeus and Demeter become pingala and ida, the positive and negative etheric nerves interpenetrating the nervous system of every individual.

Out of the union of Zeus and Demeter comes their daughter Persephone, representing the mind-soul of sentient beings. The drama of the Mysteries known as "The Rape of Persephone" depicts Persephone or mind-soul being abducted by Hades, the lord of the underworld, and carried to the lower regions of the elements. Persephone is compelled to spend four months in the lower regions and allowed to return to spend eight months in the superior—which is to say that the soul, though divine itself, is enmeshed intricately in the desires and elements of the material world. It is two-faced: one face turned toward the spirit and one face turned toward the carnal physical plane.

Zeus, the divine masculine essences, unites with Persephone, the soul force. Out of this immaculate conception a son is born— the divine Dionysus—oversoul of every mortal being.

Hera, the twin sister of Zeus, becomes the villainess in our drama. She represents the female animalistic qualities, the lowest form of negative power in the world of matter. She becomes the feminine force which, permeating Mother Nature, conspires to make the world of matter seem so real to the soul. So involved does the soul become in Hera's world of maya-illusion, it is blinded to the existence of the higher worlds.

Hera, seeing how devoted Zeus is to his offspring Dionysus, becomes jealous of the divine child—which is to say that the lower forces in the world of matter consistently war against the entrance of the divine essences into the mind-soul. Also jealous of the divine Dionysus are the animalistic Titans, housed in the lower chakras. Until resurrected, they activate the lower animalistic qualities in every soul. Everything divine in mortals is destroyed and consumed by the Titans, or diffused among the lower elements within. The only part of the soul that is safe from the destructive energies of the Titans and Hera is the divine heart center, which houses the flame of divinity—a spark of the heart of Dionysus.

In the Dionysian drama, the Titans unite with Hera to slay Dionysus. The Titans, assisted by Hera, woo Dionysus, the divine child, down into the world of matter, as has already been described. And in the struggle Dionysus is slain.

Our interpretation reveals that before the High Self of each soul gains maturity, the negative law of the lower world has power to "destroy" him or cause him to become dormant in his activities. But after Dionysus, or the heart chakra, gains full maturity—as did Dionysus in his rebirth—Hera and the Titans have no power whatever over him. He abides outside and above the negative law of the lower regions. Outside the limitations of that law he cannot be influenced by it. The Christ in every soul, represented by Dionysus, must consistently struggle against this negative law of the mundane spheres.

Continuing our discussion of the Mystery drama: Zeus, the divine monad, seeing the Christ Substance, or Dionysus, about to be completely destroyed by the Titans, saves the heart and carries it back to Mount Olympus, which conveys to us that the divine monad conceals the divine aspect of mortals in the head, or Mount Olympus, until the heart can be purified. For it is in the heart that the purification must be experienced. After saving the divine heart of Dionysus, Zeus, the masculine aspect in the divine monad, searches persistently among the lower worlds for a feminine representative worthy to mother a rebirth of his divine son. He finds it in Semele, who represents the soul's undeveloped intuitive qualities.

Zeus creates a powder of the heart of Dionysus and sends it to Semele dissolved in wine. This wine, diffused with divine properties of the cleansed heart containing the Christ Substance in its purest form, represents to us the purified and redeemed bloodstream—the blood which has been "saved" from its "sins," or cleansed of its karmic picture images.

Semele consumes the divine heart in the wine or pure bloodstream, thereby conceiving "immaculately"—which is to say that the intuitive power and the purified blood is the source of the soul's salvation ... that the Christ within can be conceived through intuition and the purified blood. This blood, the blood which has been cleansed of its karmic sins, is the "blood of the Christ," or the blood of the Christ Substance.

Semele, or intuition, not having gained full development, is easily persuaded by the negative powers of Hera to question Zeus and demand proof of his divinity. The test devised by Semele brings about her own destruction. She descends into the regions of Hades, where she becomes kundalini—the feminine serpent power lying passive at the root chakra. Zeus again saves Dionysus from sharing in Semele's destruction. He carries the yet unborn child again to the higher planes and creates an artificial womb for him in his own side.

To interpret this incident, we find: the undeveloped intuitive qualities alone, forever questioning the presence of the divine spirit within, can never bring about the birth of the Christ.

The "side" of Zeus is, in the Mysteries, the brain of humans, which is the "artificial womb" from which the Christ Body within is ultimately to be born. Kundalini must be "lifted up" to the brain centers, the "side of Zeus," before the Christ Body can be born in mortals.

Zeus, having lost his beloved Semele, brings to rebirth the divine Dionysus, the oversoul of every soul, from his side, which is to say: the divine monad ultimately brings about the birth of the Christ in every soul in the artificial womb in the brain center, after the blood has become pure and after the heart center has been cleansed of its karmic picture images.

Dionysus the Christ, though he grows to maturity, cannot attain to his full spiritual stature until he descends to the depths of Hades to rescue his blessed mother, Semele, or kundalini, the intuitive qualities sleeping in the root chakra. There Dionysus finds her, gains her release, carries her back to Mount Olympus, the head region, where she is reunited with Zeus and becomes immortal. This event dramatizes the mystery that the oversoul ultimately awakens the kundalini and, raising it to the third eye through the process of regeneration, restores the soul to its rightful place on the plane of the immortals.

The Christ in every soul and the Christ Substance in our atmospheric ethers, represented by Dionysus, must struggle against and overcome the laws of the lower mundane spheres. The Dionysian, or Christ Substance, is diffused throughout our ethers, descending from the monadic plane through the great Central Sun to reach our solar system. In the individual soul, it is centered in the forcefield of the divine oversoul above the head, descending through the sutratma to be diffused through the purified bloodstream.

In the Dionysian Mysteries, this oversoul is represented by a cluster of grapes strewn through the hair. The "vine" which extends down into humans corresponds to the sutratma and the antahkarana. As the heart seed atom is cleansed of accumulated "sins," represented by undesirable picture images, the blood-

Dionysus holding a thyrsus and a cantharus. The god is portrayed as an ephebe. Bas-relief from Herculaneum.

National Museum, Naples

stream becomes purified, allowing the Christ Substance to be diffused throughout the physical form, resulting in the birth of the Christ within.

Christian theologians, reading the literal accounts of Olympian activities, point to the immoral activities of the god Zeus, denouncing his promiscuities. To the profound mystic, however, it immediately becomes apparent that Zeus, representing the divine monad, has nothing whatever to do with human morals and ethics, but is seeking in his seemingly promiscuous activities to establish the birth of Dionysus, the Christ in every soul.

When he "abducts" different feminine consorts, uniting to create an offspring which is both divine and human, we at once recognize that this is the divine monad in action, attempting to activate the negative spiritual centers in the soul, the sole purpose being to release Semele, the kundalini, so that, springing upward, she may reunite with her immortal counterpart in the brain.*

Dionysus and Jesus

The dramas portrayed in the mammoth theaters of Greece were written by its renowned and remembered playwrights. One of the greatest of these was Euripides.

The last play written by the immortal Euripides was titled *The Bacchae*. It was his most remarkable drama, composed by the playwright in his old age after he had been sent into exile for exposing too much of the Mysteries. He chose as his exile the court of the Macedonian king. It was there he wrote *The Bacchae* and, in this play, written long before the coming of Jesus, we find a remarkable prototype of the Christ. All during his career Euripides had been disdainful of the traditional hidebound orthodoxy of his countrymen at Athens, but now, uncensored and untrammeled by the conventions of Athenian judges, he gave free reign to his genius.

*For a full and comprehensive study of these Mysteries, see the *Book of Life,* available only through Astara, 800 W. Arrow Hwy., Upland, CA 91786.

In the prologue of the play, Dionysus appears as a god to assert his divine origin after presenting a summary of his travels *in the East*. To speak of his travels in the East marks him as probably the first Mason, and certainly an initiate of the highest secrets of the Mysteries. In such initiations the candidate always "traveled east"—even as the Masons do today. Perhaps to "travel east" truly meant to come from some distant star to planet Earth—perhaps from the sun itself. Perhaps this was one of the great secrets of the early Mysteries.

Dionysus declares he has come to manifest himself in Thebes, but the countrymen of Thebes "received him not." He dared call himself the son of God, saying, "My advent is in mortal guise, from God" and he adds, "I am about to reveal my divinity to all the Thebans. I have come to Greece to institute my Mysteries there that I, a deity, may be made manifest to man."

In the play he is challenged by Pentheus, the ill-fated king of Thebes—just as the Pharisee of a later age refused to hear the truth Jesus brought and which evoked his most burning rebukes when he said, "Everyone that is of the truth heareth my voice" and "He that hath ears to hear, let him hear." Dionysus explains that he was born in a cave—as was Jesus born in a cave-stable. The "cave of initiation" is a well known recognized phrase and the initiate is always born—or born as an initiate—there. Dionysus declares that he comes as a god-man, having Zeus as his father and Semele, an Earth female, as his mother. Jesus came with God—or a "god"—as his father and with Mary, an Earth female, as his mother.

In the play there was a character by the name of Teiresias who was a blind seer. Teiresias called Dionysus "a diviner." The messenger coming from King Pentheus called him a "wonder worker." Pentheus himself called him a magician. The play depicts the arrest and subsequent trial of Dionysus which bears many points of similarity to the same incidents in the life of the great Master Jesus.

Like Jesus, Dionysus stands composed and quiet before his accusers and Pentheus, his bearing dignified. So much so, that the messenger shrinks in shame for having arrested so gallant a being, and openly disclaims responsibility for the impious deed. In the drama the messenger says to Pentheus: *This quarry—or wonder worker—was gentle to us, nor sought he to escape at all but gave his hands to us of his own free will, nor turned his complexion pale one whit but, smiling, permitted himself to be bound and led away and stood still, making our task an easy one. And I, for shame, exclaimed: "Friend I arrest you unwillingly under orders from Pentheus who dispatched me."*

Dionysus stands before Pentheus to answer the question: "What is the fashion of these Mysteries?" Dionysus replied, "Tis forbidden for the uninitiate to know," just as Jesus said, "It is not lawful for thee to hear—that which is holy must not be cast as pearls before swine."

Another direct scene from the drama may be quoted:

Pentheus: *I will keep you safe in ward (prison).*

Dionysus: *The god himself will release me when I wish.*

Pentheus: *Aye, when you invoke him standing mid your Bacchanals.*

Dionysus: *Even now he sees all, being nigh at hand.*

Pentheus: *Where is he? I see him not.*

Dionysus: *Beside me. Impiety hath dimmed your vision.*

Pentheus: *Lay hold on him. He mocks at me and Thebes.*

Dionysus: *Bind me not. A wise man among fools I go. What is not fated twill not be my fate to suffer.*

The reference Dionysus made to an invisible god standing near at hand indicates that he, like Socrates and Apollonius, was overshadowed, guided and guarded by a "daemon," a genii, a Divinity, a Prophet or a god. Dionysus calls him a god, meaning a divine spirit guide, who has the power to release him from prison and protect him from any mishap it is not his destiny to undergo.

And what of Jesus, too, when in the Garden of Gethsemane he declared himself capable of being rescued from the soldiers seeking his arrest had he so desired. One of those with Jesus struck one of the soldiers and "smote off his ear." Whereupon Jesus said: *Put up thy sword. Thinkest thou that I cannot now pray to my Father and he shall presently give me more than twelve legions of angels? But how then shall the scriptures be fulfilled, that thus it must be?* (Matthew 26:53)

In the Greek drama Teiresias, the blind seer, makes a speech very similar to that of Jesus himself at the last supper. Teiresias declares that the two primary sources of the true nourishment are bread and wine. He affirms that Dionysus himself is poured out in libation to the gods so that through him mankind may be blessed.

During the drama, while Pentheus holds Dionysus captive, his palace suddenly undergoes complete destruction. The destruction occurs immediately after the imprisonment of Dionysus, when his female disciples are loudly lamenting their grief at his capture. When, in the midst of their lamentations, they perceive the sudden destruction of the palace, they exhibit near pandemonium until suddenly Dionysus appears in the midst of them, unscathed and victorious, released from prison.

He reproaches them, saying: *So stricken with terror? Have ye fallen earthward? Then ye did not perceive the god shaking to pieces the palace of Pentheus. Rise up and be of good cheer and cease your trembling.*

Such words recall similar reproofs from the lips of Jesus to his wavering disciples when he said, "Oh, ye of little faith, wherefore did ye doubt?" And later, "Said I not unto thee that, if thou wouldst believe, thou should see the glory of God?" Again, Dionysus refers to his overshadowing "god," who caused the downfall of the palace of Pentheus and enabled Dionysus to escape his captivity.

We see throughout the Dionysian Mysteries a parallel with both Christianity and Buddhism in that both manifest the miraculous birth. Both Dionysus and Jesus attempt to point true worshipers to become, not metaphorically, but actually and literally, one with God. Both present the sacrificial death and the resurrection—the triumph of the spiritual over the material—and a new life or a new birth. All this points to the coming to Earth of a great being long ago named Dionysus and the return of a great being later named Jesus, who, having become the greatest of all initiates, gave himself unto the cross that through his sacrifice all souls of this lifewave might find the light of salvation and liberation. Then he rose in the resurrection, demonstrating the immortality not only of the soul but ultimately of the human form.

His was the greatest of all Mysteries and is beyond all comparison. He was our last great avatar and, according to his own words before ascension, he will come again to "receive us unto himself." It is toward this end that we his followers prepare, pray and teach. Indeed, it is toward his second coming that we measure the impact of our very lives—in that those of us who are forever his disciples and apostles respond freely to his admonition that "If I ascend I will draw all souls unto myself."

Chapter Eleven

The Dionysian Mysteries and the Holy Eucharist

As already described, the Dionysian Mysteries began with the allegory that while the divine Dionysus was still a child he was persuaded by the Titans to gaze into a mirror until he became fascinated by his own image. Becoming absorbed in such contemplation, he drifted downward into the lower world of matter where he was seized by the Titans. Having assumed the form of a bull, the Titans slew the bull and cut him to pieces. Thus fragmented, he became the rational soul of the world.

After slaying the young god and dismembering his body, the pieces of the bull were first boiled in water, then roasted—all of which had a symbolic interpretation. Since Dionysus represented the rational soul of the world, the dismemberment of his body was interpreted to mean that the soul of the world was broken up to be distributed throughout the mundane sphere of nature. Boiling in water symbolized the immersion of spiritual essences into the ethers or waters of the material universe. Roasting the dismembered body later symbolized the eternal union of the spiritual essences with divine fire.

When Zeus, the father of Dionysus, discovered that the Titans had scattered portions of the divine idea throughout the lower world, he slew the Titans with flashes of his thunderbolt to prevent their completely destroying divine Wisdom. From the ashes of the Titans he brought forth humankind. The purpose of evolving through the lower planes was eventually to bring the rational soul together again in the form of restored truth.

Thus each soul partakes of a fragment of the Titans as part of its lower nature, and a portion of Dionysus as its higher nature. The individual soul makes the choice during its existence in the realm of matter. The entire purpose of the Dionysian Mysteries and of initiation into those Mysteries was so that the soul could choose its god Self. Each initiate, recognizing that the soul contained both lower and higher attributes, sought initiation for the sole purpose of escaping from the Titanic influence. With full Self-realization came the truth that the soul was one in unity with the family of man and with God.

Therefore, Dionysus can only be totally resurrected when all the fragments of mankind—the souls of humanity—arrive at the state of initiation, realize their unity, one with the other, and unite to restore truth to Earth. Only then can Dionysus be made whole again. Dionysus, gazing into the mirror of matter, alludes to the attraction of sensuous life which was the cause of the young god's dismemberment.

Assembling of the thirteen scattered parts—fourteen, counting the heart—and restitution of the body symbolizes the reintegration of separate souls into the unity of One Life, just as was symbolized in the Mysteries of Osiris, whose body was also dismembered into fourteen parts and scattered throughout Egypt. The holy Eucharist, celebrated in the Church today, still represents the breaking of the body or partaking of the fragments of the divine body of Christ—another indication that Christian dogmas have their origins in the Mystery religions of antiquity. Jesus, a high initiate-Ptah of the Mysteries, knowing of the innate power of the Eucharist, introduced this mystery to his apostles at the Last Supper.

The Dionysian Architects or Artificers—an ancient secret society—were much like the Masons of today in that they were Builders sharing a secret mission of establishing architectural wonders on Earth which structurally involved the divine science of the higher planes. As already mentioned, they designed not only the structure to embody and capture the essence of Godhood, but selected the site of each monument, pyramid and cathedral to correspond with the nodes of the planet's crystal gridwork. They recognized special gridpoints as being capable of capturing and absorbing outpouring spiritual essences from celestial spheres. They recognized the ley lines of Earth. They built always to capture the grace of the Great Architect of the Universe, the Supreme Being they worshiped.

These Builders were not only builders of physical structures but initiates building the true temple of the soul, the causal body. This body, built only of the true, the good and the beautiful of each life, was the "temple not made with hands, eternal in the heavens"—built "without sound of hammer."

To offer the true interpretation of Dionysus as the wine god, it must be stated that there is an allegory which expresses that the god himself was in the wine. He *was* the wine, the wine containing the crushed heart of Dionysus, implying that the soul's divinity rests in the purification of the bloodstream through the heart chakra—and the heart seed atom. The god himself is offered in libation to the initiates. It identifies with the Eucharist of the Church which imbibes wine as the blood of Jesus. This is the true identification of the gods with the soma drink.

Thus, when Dionysus is connected with the libation of wine, it is not because he advocated revelry and drunkenness, but because he advocated partaking of the divinity of the god through the consumption of the sacred wine during the process of initiation, the wine being representative of the holy soma, which contained the esoteric properties of both the Sky God and the Earth Goddess. The Mysteries of Dionysus no more suggested drunkenness with the imbibing of the wine than do the priests today when they offer the Eucharist as the divine blood of Jesus.

In the Dionysian Mysteries, the purpose was to create spiritual ecstasy, not physical intoxication. The wine-soma drink for the initiate was potent with divine power. It contained the very essence of God Himself. So the wine of the Greater Mysteries was totally different from the wine imbibed by those who followed in the Bacchic procession, who often became physically intoxicated. They misunderstood entirely the teaching of Dionysus. Even during the procession it was originally supposed to be a matter of communing with the god.

The devotees of the Bacchic procession of the Greater Mysteries did not simply begin with a riotous dance. They prepared themselves for days before the procession. They went through a rigorous program of purification, including several days of fasting. They entered a ritual of eating a roasted morsel of flesh from a sacrificed bull, representing the sacrificed body of the god Dionysus—just as Christians today eat the bread of the Eucharist. And they drank a small powerful liquid called "wine," but which contained a secret essence of an herb such as the soma plant. They chewed ivy and laurel leaves to help them enter a spiritual trance, as did the Pythoness at Delphi. Then they began their sacred procession which led them to the temple of Eleusis or Ephesus, where they experienced the inner secret rites of initiation.

During the procession, they carried the thyrsus, which was a wand tipped with a pine cone and entwined with ivy. They twisted grapes and the vine through their hair. Over their shoulders they occasionally wore a sacred blessed fawn skin. Occasionally they wore sheep horns on their foreheads.

The procession was held at nighttime, with each devotee carrying a torch light. They were accompanied by musical instruments with the clashing of tambourines. The dances were characterized by freedom of bodily movements, such as whirling and tossing the arms and the head. The dancing itself was part of the ritual, much as the whirling dervishes of the Sufis. The dervishes whirled in order to establish a state of delirium. It was a part of their ecstatic ritual. This same practice was followed by the Dionysian initiates.

This, again, gave rise to the accusation that they danced wildly because they were all intoxicated by imbibing wine. Not true. Rather, their frenzied dancing was to initiate a state of ecstatic delirium. This, together with the very special soma drink, caused them to achieve such a state, a unique spiritual cosmic awareness. The wine of the Eucharist today is only a weak facsimile of that ancient drink.

As time went by the procession degenerated. The profane, who insisted upon imitating the candidates and who became part of the public Lesser Mysteries, entered the procession simply to indulge in physical excitement, imitating the spiritual experiences of the true initiate. Plato once said, "Many are the bearers of the thyrsus but the Bacchanals are few"—meaning that many were the imitators, but the true initiates of the Bacchic-Dionysian rites were few. Referring to the madness obtained by the true initiates, Plato also said, "Madness sent by God is better than the moderation of men." The latter part of his statement referred to the maxim carved at the entrance to the Delphic cave, "Nothing in excess."

Through the soma wine and the whirling dancing, the initiates of the Greater Mysteries attained spiritual ecstasy and made visionary contact with the god Dionysus himself, just as the Pythoness of Delphi contacted the god Apollo. Initiation established a new birth for the initiate. These initiates, after their initiation, possessed miraculous powers. They could heal diseases, control the forces of nature and even prophesy. Their new life included freedom from the restraints of civilization and the return to the simplicities of nature. They believed fervently in life after death.

They believed that at the time of their physical demise they would immediately be united with the god Dionysus whose mystical essence they had shared.

Because the rites of Dionysus experienced abuse and debasement is no reason to belittle their original true meaning. Such debasement eventually caused the higher and sublimer Eleusinian Mysteries to pass into oblivion. That condition of spiritual exultation or ecstasy, which was its principal aim, was confused with and its place usurped by "ecstasy" of quite another kind— that of physical intoxication. In both cases, ordinary consciousness is temporarily suspended. But the unconsciousness of a drunkard, stumbling over objects he cannot discern, is totally different from that of a divine or a philosopher whose inward vision is transcended so that he sees and tells of things invisible to mortal sight.

This visionary perception was the high aim of the Dionysian Mysteries. The soma drink was given to the Epoptes while the populace was given simply the wine of the grape which resulted in drunkenness and revelry. Bacchanalia, or the festivities of the Dionysian procession, became a pretext for actual licentiousness.

In the Dionysian Mysteries, we witness the miraculous birth common to Christianity and Buddhism and in fact every religion where the founder was a genuine manifestation or incarnation of God. The aim of the true initiate is to become actually one with God. Sacrificial death and resurrection—that is, the triumph of spirit over matter—represents the new life. The subject is delicate and vast. But there is no escaping the similarity of Dionysian teachings with those of Christianity—the Eucharist, with its bread and wine as partaking of the body and blood of Jesus, being an updated version of the Dionysians' imbibing the morsel of flesh and soma to partake of the fragmented form of our savior Dionysus.

Chapter Twelve

The Fall and Rebirth of the Mystery Religions

"Except a man be born from above he cannot see the kingdom of God....Art thou a Master in Israel and knowest not these things?"

Jesus is chiding Nicodemus, who has come to him stealthily in the night to learn the Mysteries and truths taught by the Master. Jesus is stating indirectly that, although Nicodemus is a high-standing official in the religion held by the Jews, he is quite ignorant of the truth of regeneration, of spiritual rebirth, of initiation, and even of life after death. This statement alone speaks vividly of Jesus' departure from orthodox Judaism and of his obvious connection with the mystical Essenes.

So is it also true in all the great religions prevalent in our modern world today—in Christianity, Islam, Hinduism, Buddhism, Judaism. Not one offers the mystery of regeneration, of a new birth, of initiation, in their doctrines of soul salvation. Yet the mystery of spiritual rebirth is the basis of all doctrines of moral reconstruction called religion. Indeed, it is the structure upon which true immortality depends—that is, the liberation of the soul from the wheel of rebirth, and the gaining of immortality after death. Thus being reborn, regenerated, means that one becomes "immortal," or "not subject to the return to mortality." Regeneration and the attainment of such liberation was the concealed truth in all the Mystery religions.

With the fall of the Mysteries humanity fell into a state of ignorance concerning, first, reincarnation and, second, escaping from the wheel of rebirth. With the fall of the Mysteries, humanity lost the understanding of reincarnation. In the new Christianity, the soul's liberation, or soul salvation, depended solely upon faith in the gentle Jesus and his ability to forgive sins, or karma, and redeem one from "eternal" punishment. Today, those of the Eastern religions understand well the cycle of rebirth, but only a scattered few understand the process of initiation and its ability to deliver the soul from the cycle of death and rebirth.

In *The Phaedo*, Plato has Socrates speaking to his disciple Cebes in a discussion concerning immortality. "Is it not a universal law," asks Socrates of Cebes, "even though we do not always express it in so many words, that opposites are generated always from one another—and that there is a process of generation from one to the other? Is it the case that everything which has an opposite is generated only from that opposite? The greater from the less? The less from the greater? The weaker from the stronger? The stronger from the weaker? The swifter from the slower? From sleep, the state of waking and the state of waking from sleep?"

"It is," replied Cebes.

"Well," said Socrates, "is there an opposite to life in the same way that sleep is the opposite of being awake?"

"Certainly," replied Cebes.

"What is it?" asked Socrates.

"Death," replied Cebes.

"Then if life and death are opposites, they are generated one from the other?"

"Yes."

"Then what is that which is generated from the living?"

"The dead," Cebes replied.

"And what is generated from the dead?" asks Socrates.

Cebes replied, "I must admit it is the living."

"Then living things and living men are generated from the dead, Cebes?"

"Clearly," said he.

"Then our souls exist after death in the other world," said Socrates.

Although Socrates is teaching of death, life after death, and rebirth, he does not point to regeneration or liberation from the wheel. To speak of life after death is only half the truth. It does not speak of true birth "from above," being born "of the spirit," of spiritual rebirth, of regeneration. Only the initiate in the caves of Eleusis, of Ephesus, of the Dionysian Mysteries, of the Orphic Rites, truly understood the meaning of regeneration, of being "born again," or born of the spirit, of soul liberation. The common feature in each of these Schools was initiation, through which the initiate gained regeneration. Though each of the Schools differed in their presentations, all offered some form of initiation through purification, probation, tests and disciplines, followed, in the Greater Mysteries, by a solemn oath of secrecy. Each claimed a founding deity and sought its benediction, its overshadowing presence and its everlasting protection.

In the Lesser Mysteries a sacred myth was established in the form of drama and ritual, even as it persists today in the Masonic Lodge. In the inner Greater Mysteries, however, the initiate gained union with the deity and attained spiritual regeneration. In the Lesser Mysteries the vision of the deity was "through a glass darkly." In the Greater, "face to face." Baptism was of utmost importance in both the Lesser and the Greater. In the waters of such purification the initiate was supposed to have died to his/her past, to have been "reborn," purified and attached to his deity, whether that deity be in the form of the oversoul, a savior, a god or a goddess. In the Eastern religions it is "Moksha" which leads the faithful toward liberation from the wheel of rebirth, for Moksha leads toward regeneration.

In the religion of ancient Egypt regeneration was the dominant theme in the Mystery religions. There was no other religion. All was based upon the Mysteries and regeneration. The Lesser Mysteries presented regeneration in the form of the yearly rebirth of the Nile, establishing it as a counterpart of the celestial river of life in Aalu, the land of the holy dead. The rebirth of Osiris in the Lesser Mystery drama was made to correspond with the rising of the Nile, bringing natural fertility and life once again to the thirsty land of Egypt.

In the Greater Mysteries the neophyte was brought to a state of rebirth through arduous preparations in the temples. Inside the deeps of the temples he entered consciously into a trance state through which he was advanced to increasing heights of illumination, until he gained liberation or salvation in the circle of the immortal gods—after which the newborn initiate devoted his/her whole will to the service of Osiris. In his trance state he met God or the gods "face to face." After his three-day journey out of the body, his soul was returned to his carefully guarded physical vehicle and he was awakened to be greeted by the band of initiates, the hierophant and the Ptah.*

The secrets of such Mysteries were set forth symbolically in *The Egyptian Book of the Dead*, which is rightfully named *The Book of the Master of the House of Hidden Places*.

Blavatsky speaks of such an initiation in the Secret Doctrine: *Let the reader turn to some most suggestive bas relief—one especially from the temple of Philae represents a scene of initiation. Two hierophants, one with the head of a hawk (the sun), the other Ibis-headed Thoth (the god of wisdom and secret learning), are standing over the body of a candidate just initiated. They are in the act of pouring a double stream of water (the water of*

*See *Initiation in the Great Pyramid* by Earlyne Chaney, available from your metaphysical bookstore or from Astara.

Rosellini

Rites of Initiation
The hierophant, wearing the mask of Anubis, bends over the en-
tranced form of the initiate experiencing the rites of initiation.

life and of new birth), the stream being interlaced in the shape of
a cross, and full of small ansated crosses.

This is allegorical of the awakening of the candidate who is
now an initiate, when the beams of the morning sun, Osiris, strike
the crown of his head, his entranced body being placed on its
wooden Tau so as to receive the rays. Then appeared the hi-
erophant-initiators, and the sacramental words were pronounced

ostensibly to the sun, Osiris— in reality, to the spirit sun within, enlightening the newly born soul.

She adds: *The passage-entrance and the sarcophagus in the King's Chamber meant regeneration. It was the most solemn symbol, a holy of holies indeed, wherein were created immortal hierophants and "sons of God." It would appear the King's Chamber could be considered to be a celestial womb. One must bend quite low in order to enter this sacred site. Once inside, the seeker, placed in the granite sarcophagus, experiences a state of trance and rebirth, emerging as a "born again" initiate. S/he has experienced a "second birth."*

The candidate for initiation was placed in a trance, during which his/her spirit-soul rose from his physical form to experience a three-day journey into the astral-spiritual world where s/he was taught the truth about death and the afterlife. The Egyptians often depicted the released soul as a bird in flight.

In *The Book of the Master* there is a potent description of a disciple watching the initiation and enthronement of his soul from the depths of the Well of Truth. He awaits in an ecstasy of yearning the moment when his oversoul, the radiant half of his being, returns from its seat of power in the upper regions of Aalu and, descending through the various symbolic transformations on the ladder of the Well of Truth, unites with the soul forever. Through such an initiation, such regeneration occurred in which the soul observes its own divinity for the first time and, through various transformations, becomes identified and united with it. Through such an initiation the disciple was taken through many steps or degrees, eliminating his "stains" and his past karma, or sins. This same initiation is described in my own book, *Initiation in the Great Pyramid.*

An initiation in the Mystery temples of Egypt was no light undertaking. Often, to fail in attainment meant death—not caused by his brother initiates but as a result of the strain of attainment and the unpreparedness of the disciple. Such an initiation was based upon the worship of Osiris and Isis—the legend of the tragic death and resurrection of Osiris, the sun god, who was known by the Egyptians to have an historical background, to actually have come from the skies to teach the Mystery religions to the Egyptians.

Such Mysteries depicted Osiris incarcerated in a chest by his scheming brother Set, who deposited the chest on the wave-tossed waters of the sea. Isis seeks to find the coffin, only to find that Set has cut his body into fourteen pieces and scattered them throughout the fourteen nomes of Egypt. Isis sets out upon a search until, still grieving, she finds the scattered pieces. A sacred temple is built over each piece, and in it funeral rites are performed. She calls for assistance from Thoth and Anubis, who, together with Isis, perform certain magical rites which restore Osiris to life. Reborn, Osiris is transplanted to the underworld, becoming lord and rewarder of the dead. The Mystery rites included the joyful return of the "Lord of Abydos" to his palace, or the return of his image to its temple.

The initiate of the Mysteries understood that Osiris stood for the divine principle in every soul. This divine principle, coffined and imprisoned in the body and tossed on the waves of material life, was revived by the love power of the soul, Isis, and, though temporarily dismembered, never loses its essential immortality.

The dismemberment of the body of Osiris symbolized the breaking of the One into the Many. The restoration of the body represented the ultimate destiny of humanity, the restoration to wholeness of the now distributed fragments of his divine self— the return of the Many to the One.

Each initiate was given the name *Osiris* and during the ceremony was addressed by this title. "As truly as Osiris lives, I also shall live. As truly as Osiris is not dead, I shall not die. As truly as Osiris is not annihilated, I shall not be annihilated." "Because I live, ye shall live also," said Jesus of Galilee many centuries later. Osiris symbolized the highest principle in man. Through initiation, the candidate sought to attain cosmic consciousness. Initiation pointed him toward that attainment in the fields of bliss called Aalu and avoided for him an Earthly rebirth.

A discourse between Hermes, a great Ptah of the Mysteries, and his disciple Tat reveals somewhat of the doctrine of regeneration. During the process of initiation Tat seeks answers to many questions from the Master Hermes, who answers: *What can I say to you, my son? I can but tell you this. When I see the simple vision brought to birth by God's mercy, I have passed through myself into a body that shall never die. And now I am not what I was before, but I am born in mind. The way to do this is not taught and it cannot be seen by the compounded element by means by which thou seeth. Thou seeth me with eyes, my son, but what I am, thou doth not understand, even with fullest strain of body and of sight.*

Tat suddenly exclaims that he can no longer behold his own familiar self—he is entering a trance state.

Hermes replies, "I would, my son, that thou hadst even passed through thyself as they who dream and sleep, yet sleepless." He then encourages Tat to seek the silence and await the mercy of God, or the "birth from above."

Tat suddenly becomes ecstatic and enters a state of cosmic consciousness: *By God made steadfast I no longer look on anything with the sight of my eyes. In heaven I am in water, air, in animals and plants. I am everywhere. Master, I see the All. I see myself in mind.* Having entered such a high estate, he is taught by Hermes the secrets, the code, imparted only to the high initiates who have experienced regeneration, or the awakening of kundalini and the opening of the third eye.*

The Fall of the Mystery Schools

When the emperors of Rome caused the downfall of the Mysteries in order to establish the growth of Christianity, the whole of their sacredness did not die. Their wisdom in exoteric form was absorbed into the new and conquering faith. In the early days, Mithraism was a serious rival, for its rites and ceremonies had spread over the entire Roman Empire. Since Christianity was building itself upon the same precepts, the rivalry between the two religions was almost fanatical. Christianity offered forgiveness and a better life here and now through the resurrected Christ.

The first generation of Christians was offered, through mystical baptism and the sacraments, a mystical union with the consciousness of their Master. His death and resurrection had insured that all who embraced his teachings might enter immortal life, which became their birthright and his supreme gift to man. Baptism to these early Christians became a form of initiation, following which the initiate, truly upreaching toward his resurrected God, brought into the common life miraculous healings and the

*See *Remembering—The Autobiography of a Mystic*, by Earlyne Chaney which describes the author's experiences in such an initiation.

gaining of spiritual perception. Each new Christian initiate reached for the powers of the new nature—the Charismata, or gifts of the spirit—the power to heal, to prophesy, to interpret, to discern.

With the passing of time, however, came the rise of institutionalism as the religion began to spread. The organization of the early Church gradually grew into a grandiose structure, governed by a hierarchy of officials, supposedly deriving a spiritual heritage from the apostles. The life of Christ presumably flowed only through the head of the spiritual organism—the pope—not by simple means of faith but through ritualistic ceremonies.

Dean Enge, writing in *Christian Mysticism*, says: *Catholicism owes to the Mysteries the notion of secrecy, of symbolism, of mystical brotherhood, of sacramental grace and, above all, of the three stages in the spiritual life: ascetic purification, illumination and Epopteia as the crown.* It was gradually becoming a Mystery religion. By the end of the fifth century the Church had adopted Mystery terms in the guise of ecclesiastical use. They had adopted separation of the baptized from the unbaptized. They had prepared the catechumens, a preparation for initiation. There was the procession to the holy of holies by the baptized who, clad in white, garlanded and crowned, bore torches toward the tabernacle. The mass clearly became the Epoptae of the Christian Mysteries. Its priesthood offered to both priest and nun awe-inspiring preparations, rituals and ceremonies, the approaches to which only the specially prepared candidate might come.

They had adopted the sacraments, or the breaking of bread and the drinking of wine, to symbolize partaking of the deity, through which a higher order of life infused the body and soul of the initiate. The bread, broken into fragments, symbolized the body of the deity, as did the dismemberment of Osiris and Dionysus in the Egyptian and Greek Mysteries.

Then came the Epiklesis, or invocation of the Holy Spirit, to transmute the bread and wine into spiritual substance and energy. To consume them was the magical moment of regeneration when the overshadowing Christ identified himself with the bread and wine and changed the inner blood and substance of the worshiper.

Christianity is thus composed of two different temperamental approaches. Some gravitate toward the Mystery religions, others to the simplicity of Jesus, accepting repentance from sins and faith in his power of redemption. One enters the Greater Mysteries. The other, the Lesser. But both involve a transformation of consciousness. Thus we see the Mystery initiations still dominating the religions of the world.

Christianity offered, through Jesus, a new commandment— "Love ye one another as I have loved you." But love cannot be compelled. This is the hardest commandment of all to follow, whether it be through the Mystery religions or through dogmatic Christianity—to love God and man with the whole being is possible only through the regenerate consciousness. The true implications of regeneration have not yet been realized or attained by Christianity. They belong to the future.

The Rebirth of the Mystery Schools

In humanity's Sixth Race now forming, of which we light seekers are a part, the glory of regeneration will seek its fulfillment. The truths and secrets of the Mysteries are again coming into birth. They will come, either through established Christianity or outside the framework of its doctrines. As the age of Aquarius comes into full blossom it begins to appear that the new age philosophies will bring to birth the secrets of regeneration, of initiation, and the secrets of true liberation from the wheel of rebirth. With these precepts and the eager outreach of would-be initiates, there may come about the fall and decline of the Christian faith, which is presently based on blind precipitation. Or some faction of Christianity may further adopt the secrets of the Greater Mysteries, which Jesus taught secretly to his twelve Apostles.

Whether inside or outside the boundaries of recognized dogma and doctrine, the reborn initiate will seek again a higher form of initiation than even that experienced in the Mysteries of antiquity—for humanity is entering a new phase of enlightenment and the hungry soul will establish again an avenue through which it might reach a higher state of attainment than that which is now available. Thus we see the rebirth of the secrets of the Mystery Schools. We see the Eucharist coming forth as a new form of initiation. We see the combination of Eastern soul-liberation and of Christian soul-salvation. We see the marriage of the Eastern and the Western faiths as the soul of the initiate seeks to merge with a higher pathway to the divine.

Perhaps Jesus himself, returning to Earth as he promised when he ascended, will establish a new truth. He promised "a new Earth and a new Man." This promise implies a new truth, a new light, a new love. One cannot give such an occurrence a title. One cannot and dare not call it "a new religion." Better would it be we label it simply "a new consciousness" and let the Lord himself call it what he will. For only he is qualified to "name" his return to us and his presence among us. We can only pray that his return be not long delayed.

A MESSAGE FROM ASTARA

The publishers of this book have made it available to you in the belief that it will make a contribution to your life on its various important levels: physical, emotional, intellectual, and spiritual.

Actually, we consider this volume to be an extension of the teachings contained in Astara's series of mystical studies known as *Astara's Book of Life*. The lessons comprising the *Book of Life* are distributed on a world-wide basis only to members of Astara. Astara was founded in 1951 as a non-profit religious and educational organization including the following concepts:

1. A center of all religions oriented to mystical Christianity but accepting all religions as beneficial to humankind.

2. A school of the ancient Mysteries offering a compendium of the esoteric teachings of all ages.

3. A fraternity of all philosophies coordinating many viewpoints of humankind and the interacting inner structures which unite us as one in the infinite.

4. An institute of psychic research with emphasis on spiritual healing of physical and mental aspects and to life before and after physical incarnation.

If these areas of interest are appealing to you, you may wish to pursue the studies of *Astara's Book of Life* as have thousands of others in some ninety countries around the world.

To give you information about Astara, its teachings, and other possible services to you, we have prepared a treatise entitled *Finding Your Place in the Golden Age*. You may have it without cost or obligation. Write:

Astara
P.O. Box 5003
Upland, CA 91785-5003

Illustrations

British Museum: Cronus, p. 26, Demeter, p. 42, Mithras, p. 48, Soul of a Scribe, p. 198.
The Louvre: Hera, p. 30, Theseus, p. 63.
Metropolitan Museum, New York: Athena, p. 32.
Belvedere Gallery, The Vatican: Apollo, p. 36 .
The Museum, Naples: Artemis, p. 35.
National Museum of Terme, Rome: Ares, p. 40.

The publisher would like to thank the following for permission to use the illustrations listed below:
Dover Publications, New York: Thoth, p. 46.
The Philosophical Research Society, Los Angeles:
Initiation Ceremony, p. 10, Consulting the Oracle, p. 96, The Rape of Persephone, p. 145.

Original artwork for Astara by Frances Paelian.
Photography by Dawn and Neal McKenzie and Anita Lintner.

7-10-10
Alexandria
Pasadena